90 Brain-Teasers For Trainers

90 Brain-Teasers For Trainers

Graham Roberts-Phelps
and
Anne McDougall

Gower

© *GRAHAM ROBERTS-PHELPS 1997*

First edition published in 1995 by Roberts-Phelps Training and Consultancy Ltd.
This edition published by
Gower Publishing Limited
Gower House
Croft Road
Aldershot
Hampshire GU11 3HR
England

Gower
Old Post Road
Brookfield
Vermont 05036
USA

Reprinted 2000

Graham Roberts-Phelps has asserted his right under the Copyright, Designs and Patents Act 1988 to be identified as the author of this work.

British Library Cataloguing in Publications Data

Roberts-Phelps, Graham
        90 brain-teasers for trainers
        1. Employees - Training of 2. Puzzles 3. Management games
        I. Title II. McDougall, Anne III. Ninety brain-teasers for
        trainers
        658.3'124

ISBN: 0 566 07979 8

Typeset in Univers by 80/20 Training Ltd and printed in Great Britain by MPG Books Ltd, Bodmin, Cornwall

CONTENTS

INTRODUCTION

BRAIN-TEASERS FOR TRAINERS is a collection of 90 **energising**, **ice-breaking**, **thought-provoking, creativity-boosting** training exercises, designed to make your training course more effective, interactive and involving.

Designed and collated by two successful independent trainers, each exercise has been carefully tried and tested in a number of different training environments.

GET YOURSELF INTO PRINT!

Do you have an activity to contribute?

The next volume of BRAIN-TEASERS FOR TRAINERS is already in production.

We would be delighted to receive contributions of suitable training activities, exercises and icebreakers. We will acknowledge all letters and any contributions that we use will contain a reference to the author and the author will receive a complimentary copy of the book.

Name:	
Position:	
Address:	
Tel:	

My training exercise or activity:

Section 1: Problem Solving

LETTER PROGRESSION

Format:	Individual
Type:	Icebreaker/Session starter
Time:	5-10 minutes
Resources:	OHP, flip-chart, training resource ref:1
Suitable for:	All levels

Purpose

To change pace or act as a break between sessions.

Procedure

Ask delegates to work individually on this simple puzzle.

Display the OHP slide.

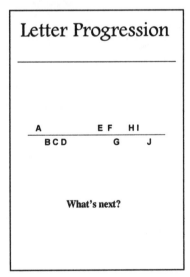

Delegates have to explain which number is next in the sequence and why.

Allow 3-5 minutes. Do not enter into any discussion.

Ask if anybody has an answer. Go around the group and ask delegates to share their ideas.

Run a short discussion on the following points.

(Answer: The progression on the top line is made up of straight lines, below the line curves.)

Discussion Points

- How many of you gave up?

- How long did it take you to find a solution?

- What lessons might we learn about how to be more creative in our approach to problem solving?

- Did anybody find a solution other than the proposed one?

- What part do our left and right brains play in problem solving?

SPOT THE DIFFERENCE

Format:	*Individual/Pairs*
Type:	*Icebreaker/Session starter*
Time:	*5-10 minutes*
Resources:	*OHP, flip-chart, training resource ref:2*
Suitable for:	*All levels*

Purpose

To practise problem solving.

Procedure

Ask delegates to work individually or in pairs on this simple puzzle.

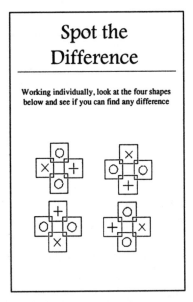

Display the OHP slide or distribute as a handout.

Delegates have to decide which, if any, are different and why.

Allow 3-5 minutes. Do not enter into any discussion.

After 5 minutes, ask if anybody has an answer and go around the group and ask delegates to share their ideas.

Run a short discussion on the following points.

(Answer: Bottom line-right hand shapes (cut out the shapes and move them around)

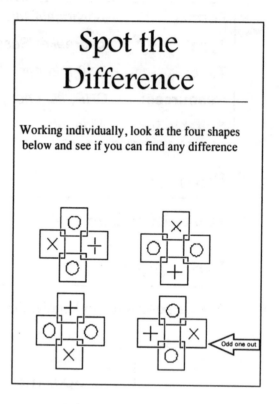

Discussion Points

➲ How many of you gave up?

➲ How long did it take you to find a solution?

➲ What lessons might we learn about how to be more creative in our approach to problem solving?

➲ Did anybody find a solution other than the proposed one?

HEADS OR TAILS

Format:	Pairs/Individual
Type:	Icebreaker
Time:	5-10 minutes
Resources:	OHP, flip-chart, training resource ref: 3
Suitable for:	All levels

Purpose

To identify learning opportunities and ambitions.

Procedure

Group delegates in pairs or ask them to work individually, depending on the size of the group.

Distribute as a handout, or display as an OHP slide.

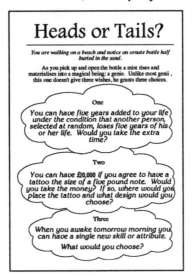

Read out and review instructions with delegates, making sure all are clear on the instructions, particularly the last section:

When you awake tomorrow morning you can have a single new skill or attribute. What would you choose?

(Although the 'tattoo' question might prompt more fun!)

After 5-10 minutes have elapsed, ask each delegate in turn to present their answers to the main group.

List these on the flip-chart.

Discussion Points

- Do we ever stop and think how much we have learnt and how much we already know?

- What skills do we need to succeed in the future?

- What skills and knowledge do we learn as part of our daily lives?

SPROUTS

Format:	*Pairs/Individuals*
Type:	*Icebreaker*
Time:	*15-20 minutes*
Resources:	*OHP, training resource ref: 4*
Suitable for:	*All levels*

Purpose

To get delegates working together in an interesting and creative way.

Procedure

This activity is based on a fascinating and easy-to-learn game developed by mathematician John Conway, called Sprouts.

The playing surface is a group of sixteen dots arranged in a four by four grid.

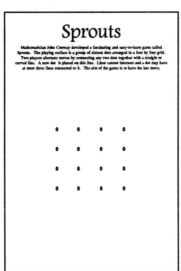

Two players alternate moves by connecting any two dots together with a straight or curved line. A new dot is placed on this line.

Lines cannot intersect and a dot may have at most three lines connected to it. The aim of the game is to have the last move.

The game produces many interesting patterns. While some people draw short stark lines, others draw long flowing lines. Some people reach far out with their moves, others play close in. As a result a sprout game can become an aesthetic endeavour as well as a battlefield for the intellect.

People can quickly become fascinated by the strategic challenge presented by the game.

Distribute the handout and review the instructions with the group.

Divide delegates into pairs and set a time limit. Delegates must move quickly.

Option: You could run the exercise as a knock-out tournament, with rounds at various times during a longer course.

Discussion Points

○ Do different people have different approaches and tactics?

○ Does any one particular approach ensure success?

○ Did you find yourself becoming absorbed in the game?

○ Did routes suddenly appear when you thought none existed?

EXERCISING YOUR VISUAL MEMORY

Format:	Group
Type:	Icebreaker/Problem solving
Time:	10-15 minutes
Resources:	OHP, training resource ref: 5, 6, 7, 8, 9
Suitable for:	All levels

Purpose

To stretch memory muscles and practise visual recognition and retention.

Procedure

Read out and review instructions with delegates.

Study the following figures for a short time and then draw them as accurately as you can from memory.

Make sure that everybody is clear on what to do.

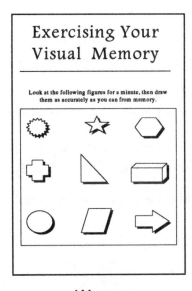

Warm up

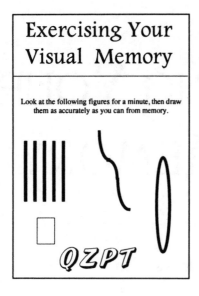

Very easy

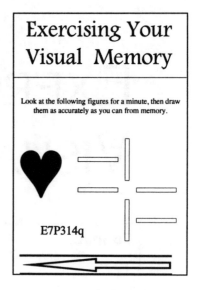

Easy

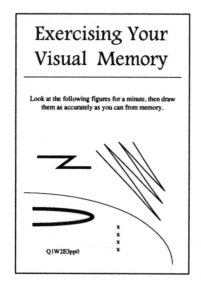

Hard

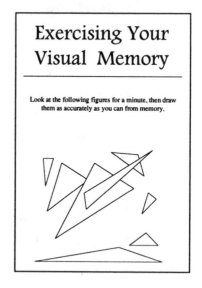

Very hard

Display the OHP slides for **one minute only** for the group to study. (Alternatively distribute face up as a handout.)

Turn off the OHP or ask delegates to turn the handout face down and draw the pictures from memory.

(Five different diagram sheets are included, each of varying complexity. These can be used at different times during a course.)

Repeat for each of the different sheets.

Discussion Points

- Did you remember more or less than you expected?

- Which diagrams did you remember best?

- Did you remember more as time passed?

- What techniques or methods did you use to help you remember?

Thinking as Sequencing

Format:	*Pairs/Syndicates*
Type:	*Problem solving/logical thinking*
Time:	*25-35 minutes*
Resources:	*OHP, flip-chart, training resource ref: 10*
Suitable for:	*Managers, supervisors, team leaders*

Purpose

To explore how we approach different decision-making and thinking processes.

Procedure

Form delegates into small syndicates.

Thinking as Sequencing

One aspect of problem solving and analysis is how we divide up a large complex plan of action into a series of simpler actions. For example, select three of the following and write out the steps you need to perform to achieve these projects. List possible alternatives if things don't go according to plan.

- ✓ Making your first million
- ✓ Training and keeping a pet monkey
- ✓ Travelling to China on a bicycle
- ✓ Learning competition-level tennis
- ✓ Becoming fluent in a foreign language
- ✓ Becoming a clothes designer for a rock band
- ✓ Building an extension to your home
- ✓ Building your own home
- ✓ Rewiring your house or flat
- ✓ Putting a new bathroom in your house
- ✓ Going on holiday or overseas trip
- ✓ Starting a newspaper
- ✓ Designing a restaurant

Distribute as a handout, or display as an OHP slide.

Introduce the activity by saying that one aspect of problem solving and analysis is how we divide up a large, complex plan of action into a series of simpler actions. Some of us do this in a methodical manner, others in a more random fashion. Also some factors would be of varying importance to each of us. For example, consider how we might go about buying and using a home computer. (Run a short discussion if you wish.)

Read out and review the instructions with delegates, making sure all are clear on what is to be done.

'Select one of the following and write out the steps you need to perform to achieve these projects. List possible alternatives if things don't go according to plan.'

Ask delegates to work in a group arriving at an outline plan by consensus, noting any differences in approach. Set a time limit of 10-15 minutes, or longer if time is available.

After the time has elapsed, ask each group in turn to elect a spokesperson and present their plan to the main group.

Discussion Points

● How does our approach in our daily work follow the sequences presented?

● How much of our problem solving and planning is organised, and how much random or lateral?

● When would sequence thinking be most useful?

NINE DOTS PROBLEM

Format:	Pairs/Individuals
Type:	Icebreaker/Problem solving
Time:	15-20 minutes
Resources:	OHP, flip-chart, training resource ref: 11
Suitable for:	All levels

Purpose

To demonstrate how we constrain our thinking, that is our lack of ability to find solutions to problems because of our self-imposed assumptions.

Procedure

This really is a classic, and regular course-attendees will usually have encountered it before, although most delegates will not. (Those that have, often forget!). *(Authors' note: While it might be familiar to some readers, as it was the inspiration for this book, it could not be excluded.)*

Distribute the handout, display as an OHP or draw the nine dots in a square on the flip-chart.

Nine Dots

Connect the nine dots below using only four straight lines, without taking your pen off the paper.

```
o       o       o


o       o       o


o       o       o
```

Read instructions *'Connect all nine dots using only four straight lines, without taking your pen off the paper.'*

Avoid entering any discussion about methods, simply repeat instructions.

After ten minutes or when all delegates have solved the problem (unlikely), invite a successful delegate to draw the solution on the flip-chart.

Discussion points:

○ How many of you gave up after only a few minutes?

○ How many of you tried to rewrite or 'bend' the rules?

○ Why did it seem relatively obvious once the solution had been discovered or displayed?

○ What can this exercise tell us about our own approach to problem solving and changing how to do things?

○ What problems or challenges are you currently facing, or have recently encountered, where simply 'looking outside of the square' could highlight a solution? (Our own assumptions can often be the block to a solution rather than the problem itself.)

Answer:

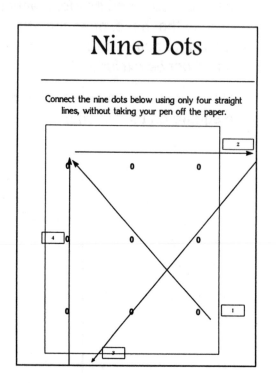

FORCE OF HABIT

Format:	Group
Type:	Icebreaker
Time:	5 minutes or less
Resources:	Training resource ref: 12
Suitable for:	All levels

Purpose

To identify and recognise how consistent we are in our behaviours and our resistance to change.

Procedure

Distribute as a handout, or display as a slide.

Force of Habit

Please complete the following:

Sign your name here as you would normally do:

Now place the pen or pencil in the OPPOSITE hand to that which you normally use and sign your name again.

Allow delegates a few seconds, making sure everybody signs their name using alternate hands, even if you have to offer some direct encouragement.

(It is curious to note how some people, perhaps 10-15 per cent of a group are *extremely* reluctant to perform even this simple change operation!)

(An alternative or additional exercise is to ask delegates to sit in a different seat next to two different colleagues when returning from a break. After everybody is sitting down, draw delegates' attention to the resistance or reluctance that was either felt or expressed.)

Discussion Points

○ How did that feel?

○ Why did some of you resist even such a small, one-off, change of habit?

○ Apart from how difficult this might have been, consider how "strange" and uncomfortable this seemed. You could easily learn to sign your name with either hand, usually far faster than you might think, however the resistance to change may take longer to overcome.

Optional: *Discuss with your colleagues how much a 'creature of habit' you are:*

○ Do you travel the same way to work every day? Take lunch at the same time? Eat the same foods? Do the same things at weekend?

○ Watch the same programmes or channels on television?

Consider why this is.

THE POWER OF QUESTIONS

Format:	*Volunteer from group*
Type:	*Icebreaker*
Time:	*5 minutes*
Resources:	*Pack of cards*
Suitable for:	*All levels*

Purpose

An amusing icebreaker that highlights the use of rapport and leading questions.

Procedure

Important: For best results, take time to practise this little trick with friends *before* performing it on a course.

Select a volunteer and ask one of the group to pick a card from a normal pack of playing cards. Only you and him or her should see this card.

Place the card face down on the desk.

Turn to another volunteer delegate and ask them a series of either/or questions. By carefully and subtly choosing the option you want you are able to lead them to the card that is on the desk.

Example: (Card is the three of hearts)

Q: This pack has two colours, red and black, please choose red or black.

(If they choose red 'Good, now red is made-up of hearts and diamonds, choose...' However, if they choose black 'Good, that leaves red...')

Q: The red suits are hearts and diamonds, please choose hearts or diamonds.

Divide and talk through the pack using questions covering such aspects as:

Face cards/numbers.

Low/ high numbers Ace-5/6-10.

Three or four.

Discussion Points

- How did I lead the other person to say the card I wanted?

- Did it really matter that they chose one of the options I suggested?

- Did it feel a bit forced or 'pushy'?

- How could you have done it more subtly? (Using it within a conversation?)

PARIS IN THE SPRING

Format:	Group
Type:	Icebreaker/Subject starter
Time:	5 minutes
Resources:	OHP, flip-chart, training resource ref: 13
Suitable for:	All levels

Purpose

To demonstrate that we make assumptions and jump to conclusions quickly, often without seeing the true picture.

Procedure

Display the OHP and ask delegates to read it.

After a few seconds, turn off the OHP and ask delegates to tell you what it said in the triangle.

Gain a response from all delegates until somebody gives you the correct answer, (there are two 'ins').

If nobody is right, ask them to try again as they are all wrong.

Notice the confusion and puzzlement.

After a short time, redisplay the OHP and let delegates find the right answer themselves.

Discussion Points

- Why didn't we see the 'right' words first time?

- How do our assumptions shape our perceptions?

- Do we believe what we see or see what we believe?

- How do we know that our perceptions and assumptions of our customers and organisations are correct ones?

- Could they be incorrect or inaccurate?

THE PARAGRAPH PUZZLER

Format:	*Pairs/Individuals*
Type:	*Icebreaker*
Time:	*5-10 minutes*
Resources:	*OHP, flip-chart, training resource ref: 14*
Suitable for:	*All levels*

Purpose

To test our powers of perception, awareness and thinking.

Procedure

Distribute the handout or display on an OHP.

Paragraph Puzzler

"George looked out over the fields, only to see three young children climbing the hedge into the sheep's pen. "Oi!" he yelled loudly "Get yourselves out of there!" But his shouts went unnoticed by the children. Jumping down from his jeep, he set off over the muddy field in the direction of the sheep.

Whilst the ploughed field would be tricky for most people to run on, he quickly got to the hedge next to the sheep. His sudden presence rooted thechildren to the spot in surprise. "Hey you kids, you'll frighten them sheep, now get out of there!" Without further thought, they took to their heels, not stopping until they got to the next field."

Question: *What is unusual about this passage?*

Delegates can either work in pairs or individually.

Set delegates a time limit of about five minutes to find out what is unusual about this paragraph, after this time they should each give you an answer.

Avoid entering into discussion or answering questions; rather, direct delegates to trust their own judgement and reasoning.

After five minutes, go around the room, collecting conclusions. Do not comment on any until all answers are given.

Explain that the answer is that it does not contain the letter 'a', the most common letter in the English language. Delegates may also find other things, which are not apparent to others or even invented.

Discussion Points

- How did you approach the problem?

- Did any of you give up?

- Did you make wild guesses or use a logical approach?

- Did any of you look for more complex or detailed answers and perhaps over-look the more obvious?

SWOT ANALYSIS

Format:	Pairs/Syndicates
Type:	Thinking/Planning
Time:	30-40 minutes
Resources:	OHP, flip-chart, training resource ref: 15
Suitable for:	All levels

Purpose

To identify personal and company strengths, weaknesses, opportunities for improvement and real or potential threats.

Procedure

Introduce the exercise by asking if anybody has ever heard of a SWOT chart or SWOT analysis.

Explain that it is a method used by management specialists and business planners to gain a strategic perspective of personal and company strengths, weaknesses, opportunities for improvement and real or potential threats.

Even if delegates are familiar with the concept and have done a SWOT chart before, unless that is very recently, stress that it is valuable to do so regularly as things do change, including our judgements and perspectives.

Display the SWOT chart on an OHP or distribute as a handout.

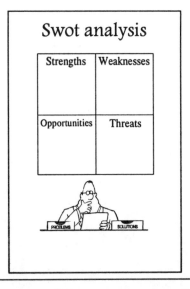

Ask delegates to work in groups of 2 or 3 and to complete the matrix for their organisation or division in relation to_____(select your own topic. You could focus the direction as you wish: e.g. marketing, management, people, safety, etc.)

Distribute the matrix as a handout.

Allow 15-20 minutes

After about 15 minutes regain the groups' attention and go around the room asking each group to read out or present their Strengths, Weaknesses, Opportunities and Threats.

Develop any points that arise, and summarise these on the flip-chart.

Discussion points

- Quite often the same elements can be both strengths and weaknesses. Why is this?

- Are our weaknesses of our own creation?

- Of those listed and discussed so far, which do you believe is our single greatest strength?

- Of those listed and discussed so far, which do you believe is our single greatest weakness?

- Of those listed and discussed so far, which do you believe is our single greatest threat?

- Of those listed and discussed so far, which do you believe is our single greatest opportunity?

- Are there any actions we can take to maximise or minimise these?

Section 2: Number Crunching

NUMERIC PROGRESSION/1

Format:	*Individual*
Type:	*Icebreaker/Session starter*
Time:	*5-10 minutes*
Resources:	*Flip-chart, OHP, training resource ref: 16*
Suitable for:	*All levels*

Purpose

To change pace or act as a break between sessions.

Procedure

Ask delegates to work individually on this simple number puzzle.

Write the following on the flip-chart or display on the OHP:

Numeric Progression/1

Working in groups of two or three, continue the progression and find a way to explain this. After five minutes elect one delegate to present your solution to the rest of the group.

3 1 2 8 3 1 3 0 ...

Delegates have to continue and explain the number progression.

Allow 2-3 minutes only.

Ask if anybody has an answer, go around the group and ask delegates to share their ideas.

Run a short discussion on the following points.

Discussion Points

- Who looked at the numbers individually, rather than in 2s?

- How long did it take you to find a solution?

- Did anybody find a solution other than the proposed one?

- How does the way we view something affect its meaning or solution?

Answer :

3132

NUMERIC PROGRESSION/2

Format:	*Individual*
Type:	*Icebreaker/Session starter*
Time:	*5-10 minutes*
Resources:	*Flip-chart, OHP, training resource ref: 17*
Suitable for:	*All levels*

Purpose

To change pace or act as a break between sessions.

Procedure

Ask delegates to work individually on this simple number puzzle.

Write the following on the flip-chart:

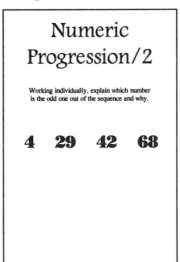

Numeric
Progression/2

Working individually, explain which number
is the odd one out of the sequence and why.

4   29   42   68

Delegates have to explain which number is the odd number out of the sequence and why.

Allow 3-5 minutes. Do not enter into any discussion.

Ask if anybody has an answer. Go around the group and ask delegates to share their ideas.

Run a short discussion on the following points.

Discussion Points

- How many different 'solutions' did you find?

- How long did it take you to find a solution?

- Did anybody find a solution other than the proposed one?

- How does the way we view something affect its meaning or solution?

Answer:

The correct answer is that 4 is the odd number out, all the others come with rice and 4 is Barbecue Spare Ribs! ...*wait for the groan.*

MATHS MAGIC/1

Format:	*Pairs/Individuals*
Type:	*Icebreaker*
Time:	*3-5 minutes*
Resources:	*Flip-chart*
Suitable for:	*All levels*

Purpose

A simple icebreaker to show how numbers can be used to present what we want them to mean, and develop a theme of curiosity.

Procedure

Perform the following calculation on the flip-chart, prompting delegates for answers:

Q: **How many days are there in a normal year?**

        - 365

Q: **How many weeks in a year?**

        - 52

Q: **So, with seven days in a week, 52 x 7 should equal 365?**

        Do you agree?

Ask a delegate to check the calculation, and you will find that it **only comes to 364!**

MATHS MAGIC/2

Format:	*Group*
Type:	*Icebreaker*
Time:	*5 minutes*
Resources:	*Flip-chart*
Suitable for:	*All levels*

Purpose

A simple icebreaker to show how easily numbers can be confusing and not what they first appear.

Procedure

Ask a member of the group or audience the following questions, as quickly as possible:

Q:　　　**What number comes after ninety nine?**

　　　　They should reply 100.

Q:　　　**What comes after nine hundred and ninety nine?**

　　　　They will probably answer 1000.

Now **quickly** ask **What comes after nine thousand and ninety nine?**

　　　　They will probably answer 10,000.

Wrong! The answer is 9100.

Discussion Points

○ How often do we hear what we want to hear or what we expect, rather than what is really said?

MATHS MAGIC/3

Format:	*Pairs/Individuals*
Type:	*Icebreaker*
Time:	*3-5 minutes*
Resources:	*Flip-chart*
Suitable for:	*All levels*

Purpose

A simple icebreaker to show how numbers can be used to confuse.

Procedure

Read out the following numbers, asking delegates to perform some simple arithmetic in their heads.

1000

20

1000

30

1000

40

1000

10

Ask delegates to write down or shout their answer.

How many people made it 5000?

8 out of 10 people do. The correct answer is 4100!

NUMBER JUMBLE

Format:	*Pairs/Syndicates*
Type:	*Session starter/Icebreaker*
Time:	*5-10 minutes*
Resources:	*OHP, flip-chart, training resource ref: 18*
Suitable for:	*All levels*

Purpose

To explore our capacity for memory and juggling numbers.

Procedure

First, form delegates into groups of around 4 people.

Introduce the activity by saying that studies have shown that there are definite limits to our attention span. We can concentrate only so long on something before our mind skips on to something else. Another limitation is that we can juggle only so many items in our minds at any one time.

To demonstrate this, try the following exercise:

Read each of the following series of numbers to yourself. After each series, close your eyes, and repeat the numbers or write them down. Which is the longest series you can hold in your mind?

Display the OHP slide to the group, revealing one line of numbers at a time.

Number Jumble

Read each of the following series of numbers to yourself.
After each series, close your eyes, and repeat the numbers or
write them down.

Which is the longest series you can hold in your mind?

3 5 4 8 4

5 7 9 1 3 2

2 5 4 7 7 0 4

8 5 7 1 3 2 7 0

2 4 6 5 8 4 2 4 5

1 2 6 1 9 4 1 7 2 1 1 9 6 9

When all the numbers have been attempted, reveal each line again, asking delegates to score two points for each correct number in the correct sequence, one point for the correct number out of sequence.

Discussion Points

➡ If you're like most people, you may find that juggling five numbers in your head is manageable.

➡ Seven numbers becomes fairly difficult and fourteen numbers seems to be impossible. Psychologists suggest that most of us can carry, at most, about seven discrete bits of information at once. We can deal fairly easily with a seven-digit telephone number, with seven countries in a continent, with seven new people in a meeting. Any more than that and we need either to write things down or to rearrange the information in a more manageable way.

MENTAL STAYING POWER/1

Format:	*Group*
Type:	*Thinking practice*
Time:	*5-10 minutes*
Resources:	*OHP, flip-chart, training resource ref: 19*
Suitable for:	*All levels*

Purpose

To practise our mental agility and stamina.

Procedure

Introduce the activity by saying that in this modern age of calculators, computers and digital toys, our brains have less to do in many respects.

This simple exercise reawakens some of the natural skills and agility that we developed during our education but perhaps use less frequently now.

Display the OHP slide and read out the instructions to delegates, making sure all are clearly understood.

Mental Staying Power/1

In your head, count the number of capital letters of the alphabet that contain curved lines.

Start now.

Ask them to write the answer down when they have it.

(Make a note of who is first, second etc.)

Wait until everybody or nearly everybody has finished the exercise before asking for and checking answers.

Answer: 11

Discussion Points

- How far did you get?

- What techniques did you use? Visualisation?

- How hard was it concentrate?

- Can you learn better concentration skills?

MENTAL STAYING POWER/2

Format:	*Group*
Type:	*Thinking practice*
Time:	*5-10 minutes*
Resources:	*OHP, flip-chart, training resource ref: 20*
Suitable for:	*All levels*

Purpose

To practise our mental agility and stamina.

Procedure

This simple exercise tests our brain's ability to perform simple mathematics, something that we do much less frequently due to the many high-technology aids in our world.

Distribute the handout and display as an OHP. Read out the instructions to delegates, making sure all are clear on what to do.

Mental Staying Power/2

Once upon a time in ancient Rome, a peasant farmer saved the life of the son of a very wealthy land owner during a dispute over a local matter. In gratitude, the wealthy man offered the peasant any reward he could name. The farmer replied that he would like the landowner to place a one-penny piece on a chess board, and then have it doubled for every square on the board. The landowner roared with laughter at the simpleton's ridiculous request and agreed straight away. But was this as daft as it sounds?

How much did the farmer receive from the man?

Performing the calculation in their heads. You may keep a tally of boxes or doubles completed.

The objective is to try to complete the puzzle, with the first person to arrive at the correct answer being declared the winner.

Delegates should write down the answer or number, performing the calculation in their heads. You may keep a tally of boxes or doubles completed.

(Make a note of who is first, second etc.)

Wait until everybody or nearly everybody has finished the exercise before asking for and checking answers.

Answer: 9,223,372,037,000,000,000 pennies.

Discussion Points

➡ How far did you get?

➡ What techniques did you use? Visualisation?

➡ How hard was it to concentrate?

➡ Can you learn better concentration skills?

PRESTIDIGITATION

Format:	Pairs/Individuals
Type:	Problem solving
Time:	5-10 minutes
Resources:	OHP, training resource ref: 21
Suitable for:	All levels

Purpose

To practise our mathematical agility and quick thinking.

Procedure

This simple exercise tests our brain's ability to perform simple mathematics, something that we do much less frequently due to the many high technology aids in our world.

(A definition of prestidigitation is sleight of hand, nimble fingered, tricks.)

The exercise is based on a popular number puzzle in which you must use all the digits from one to nine and any combination of plus signs and minus signs to add up to 100.

The digits must also remain in their original sequence.

Display the OHP slide and make sure everybody is clear on the instructions.

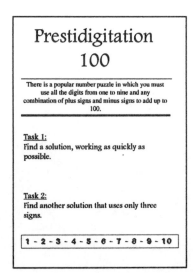

Prestidigitation
100

There is a popular number puzzle in which you must use all the digits from one to nine and any combination of plus signs and minus signs to add up to 100.

Task 1:
Find a solution, working as quickly as possible.

Task 2:
Find another solution that uses only three signs.

1 - 2 - 3 - 4 - 5 - 6 - 7 - 8 - 9 - 10

Instruct delegates to complete both tasks, working as quickly as possible, either in pairs or individually. Ask delegates to indicate when they have finished the first and then second task, noting the first few to finish.

Answers:

Task 1: One possible solution is this: 12 + 3 - 4 + 5 + 67 + 8 + 9 = 100. This solution contains six signs, five plus signs and one minus sign.

Task 2: (Can you find another solution that uses only three signs?) A possible solution is: 98 - 76 + 3 x 4 =100.

Discussion Points

- How many tries did you take to solve the problem?

- What approach did you take?

- Was it easier or harder than you first thought?

Section 3: Communication Skills

LANGUAGE AND MEANING

Format:	*Individual/Group*
Type:	*Icebreaker/Session starter*
Time:	*20-30 minutes*
Resources:	*Flip-chart, training resource ref: 22*
Suitable for:	*All levels*

Purpose

To introduce delegates or to develop further understanding of communication and interpersonal skills.

Procedure

Ask delegates to work individually.

Distribute the handout and ask delegates to complete it by writing down their response to the questions on the worksheet.

Language and Meaning

Give your definition of the following words or phrases.
What do they mean to you?
How might others understand them?

- Annoying -
- Relax! -
- No problem! -
- I won't be a minute -
- Unfortunately...-
- With due respect... -
- Off the record...-
- I would be grateful if you could please...-
- Can I help you...? -
- Have a nice day...? -
- To be honest... -
- We're looking into it... -
- That's an interesting point -
- I'll be in touch -
- We must have lunch sometime -
- I have instructed to tell you... -
- The cheque's in the post -

Allow 5-10 minutes to complete.

When all delegates have finished, compare responses on the flip-chart and run a short discussion around the following points.

Discussion Points

○ Why were there different responses to the same question?

○ What role did the words themselves play in this outline?

○ What role did your past experience have?

○ How did you decide on your answers?

○ What can we learn from this about everyday communication?

LIE DETECTOR TEST

Format:	*Group*
Type:	*Icebreaker/Communication skills*
Time:	*40-45 minutes*
Resources:	*Flip-chart, training resources ref: 23, 24*
Suitable for:	*All levels*

Purpose

This exercise is an interesting icebreaker and session starter or can be run as a test of delegates' communication, presentation and listening skills (not to mention how well they can lie).

Procedure

Introduce the exercise by asking delegates to rate themselves on how well they think they can lie, and also how well they detect when somebody else is being deceitful.

Next, ask for three volunteers, perhaps including somebody who thinks they are a very good 'persuader' (liar!) and somebody who is less confident.

Explain to the group that each of these three 'suspects' will be interviewed twice regarding their activities and whereabouts last weekend. At one interview each 'suspect' will be completely and absolutely truthful, at the other they will be completely untruthful and only the 'suspect' will know which one.

The suspects' goal is to mislead the group into believing that the false account is the truthful account.

Distribute the handout to the suspects and the observer's sheet to the rest of the group. Allow suspects 4-5 minutes to prepare individually out of the room. Ask the remaining delegates to think about or discuss what they will be looking or listening for.

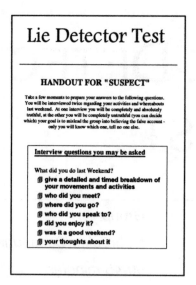

Lie Detector Test

HANDOUT FOR "SUSPECT"

Take a few moments to prepare your answers to the following questions. You will be interviewed twice regarding your activities and whereabouts last weekend. At one interview you will be completely and absolutely truthful, at the other you will be completely untruthful (you can decide which) your goal is to mislead the group into believing the false account - only you will know which one, tell no one else.

Interview questions you may be asked

What did you do last Weekend?
- give a detailed and timed breakdown of your movements and activities
- who did you meet?
- where did you go?
- who did you speak to?
- did you enjoy it?
- was it a good weekend?
- your thoughts about it

Lie Detector Test

Observer's Sheet

Please make notes in the spaces provided during the interview. Leave your conclusions until you have seen both interviews.

Suspect name_____

Interview A	Interview B

This suspect was lying on interview _____

Suspect name_____

Interview A	Interview B

This suspect was lying on interview _____

Suspect name_____

Interview A	Interview B

This suspect was lying on interview _____

Interview suspects one at time, for about 3-4 minutes each. Interview all three once, and then repeat. Be careful to use similar questions each time and continue until all suspects have been interviewed twice.

Allow delegates a few minutes to finish completing the summary box and then collect sheets in. Summarise results as a whole on the flip-chart and ask suspects to reveal at which interview they had been telling the truth.

Discussion Points

- How did you know when someone was lying, if indeed you did?

- Who was most convincing in deceiving the group?

TRAINING COURSE RULES

Format:	*Syndicates*
Time:	*15-20 minutes*
Resources:	*OHP, flip-chart, training resources ref: 25,26*
Suitable for:	*All levels*

Purpose

This is really just a short activity to set a frame for delegates' interaction and involvement in a course or training session.

Procedure

(This activity is useful when training people for the first time, or for those who are perhaps attending their first training course for a while.)

It is assumed that you will agree with the 'rules' and your training style is interactive and focused on skill development through role play, interaction and skill practice sessions.

Introduce the OHP slide as being an exercise to establish a few guidelines in setting a frame for delegates' interaction and involvement in a course or training session.

Course 'Rules'

1. Have fun - create
2. Create choices wherever possible
3. With risk comes reward
4. We learn best by
5. We are learning for real life
6. Take responsibility for your own learning

After 10-15 minutes ask syndicates to list their points on a flip-chart and review them with the rest of the group. You might choose to post these around the room.

NB: In true 'Blue Peter' fashion, you may choose to show the slide as 'one you made earlier'. The extra notes are included as well (see Appendix).

Review each point: some notes are included.

ONE-WAY COMMUNICATION

Format:	Main group
Type:	Communication
Time:	15-20 minutes
Resources:	OHP, flip-chart, training resource ref: 27
Suitable for:	All levels

Purpose

To highlight the need to establish two-way communication and use non-verbal as well as verbal communication techniques.

Procedure

Select two delegates and ask them to sit opposite each other across the room, facing away from each other, or in front of the rest of the group, so that one cannot see the other or what they are writing. (This exercise can be done one to one or alternatively you can ask one volunteer to read descriptions to the whole group.)

Give one delegate the handout and ask them, without using any visual aids or gestures, to describe what is shown on the page so that others can draw it.

After 3-4 minutes, or when the exercise is completed, run a short discussion around the following questions.

Summarise by empathising that the essence of effective communication is being able to test understanding and summarise. Also, being sure to use language and references that are easily understood helps the other person best.

Discussion Points

○ What would have made the exercise easier?

○ How else could you have communicated the 'message'?

○ What does this tell us about how we use our own communication skills on a daily basis?

○ What can we learn and apply from this exercise?

Self-Assessment Questions

Format:	*Individual*
Type:	*Self-assessment and team building*
Time:	*20 minutes*
Resources:	*None, training resources ref: 28, 29, 30,31*
Suitable for:	*All, especially managers and professionals*

Purpose

This activity is designed to help delegates develop the skills of self-measurement and self-assessment. It also practises self-disclosure in a team environment.

Procedure

This is a good exercise to change pace in a training environment. After a great deal of group or syndicate work, it will allow delegates to work individually and quietly on their own, reflecting on their own strengths and weaknesses.

Introduce the exercise as being an opportunity to become more self-aware and look at your own strengths and weaknesses objectively.

Distribute handouts to delegates and ask them to work through the questions carefully and thoughtfully, taking time to think through the questions and being as honest as possible. There are four questionnaires which can be completed individually, at the same time or as a sequence.

Self-Assessment Questions/1

1. Briefly, how do you view your role in your current position?

2. If you could have any position or job you wanted, what would you do?

3. What qualities do you feel you have that are most valuable to the company?

4. What qualities do you have that you feel are currently underused?

5. If you could live your life again, what changes would you make?

Self-Assessment Questions/2

1. What do you think makes the difference between success and failure in your business or profession?

2. What do you feel has been your greatest accomplishment in your life?

3. What has been your greatest disappointment?

4. What have you done in the past year to improve yourself?

5. How do you visualise your future?

Self-Assessment Questions/3

1. How important is money to you?

2. How does your spouse feel about your job and how interested are they in the company?

3. What are your pet hates, the things that upset you the most?

4. What do most people often criticise you for?

5. What do you most often criticise others for?

Self-Assessment Questions/4

1. What factors in your past have contributed most to your own development?

2. What factors in your past have been handicaps in preventing you from moving ahead more quickly?

3. Who do you consider to be the most successful person you have ever met? -Why?

4. Describe your life and the things around as you would like them to be in ten years' time.

5. What really motivates you?

Delegates should be ready to read out or present their answers to the group.

Allow 5-10 minutes per questionnaire.

Group review may be difficult because of the personal nature of the questions, although a structured discussion around key questions may be useful to prompt contributions.

Discussion points

➲ Which questions were the hardest to answer?

➲ Are there any answers that surprised you?

INSTANT PERSUASION

Format:	*Pairs/Syndicates*
Type:	*Session starter/Icebreaker*
Time:	*15-20 minutes*
Resources:	*OHP, flip-chart, training resource ref: 32*
Suitable for:	*All levels*

Purpose

A lively and interesting activity to experiment with different commendation styles and techniques.

Procedure

Divide delegates into pairs.

Distribute the handout, display as an OHP or draw on a flip-chart.

Instant Persuasion

You have three minutes to persuade another group member to do something which would be good for him or her (e.g.. miss lunch, lose weight, take up aerobics, read a certain book, watch less television). Use a high-pressure style. The other person may resist and, if persuaded, must actually carry out the action to which he or she agreed. Take a few minutes to collect your thoughts and make some notes:

Objective:

Notes:

Review the instructions with the delegates and make sure everybody is clear on what to do.

'You have three minutes to persuade another group member to do something which would be good for him or her (e.g. miss lunch,

lose weight, take up aerobics, read a certain book, watch less television).

Use a high-pressure style.

The other person may resist and, if persuaded, must actually carry out the action to which he or she agreed.'

Avoid entering any discussion about methods simply repeat the instructions.

After 10 or 15 minutes or when all the delegates have attempted the task, go round the room asking delegates whether or not they were successful.

Run a discussion around the points below.

Discussion Points

- How effective was this approach?

- When does it or when would it work best?

- If your approach failed, why do you think this was?

- What style might have been more successful?

- Did any attempts end in deadlock or agreement?

- How did you feel being persuaded in this way?

- Would any agreements reached have been lasting?

MAKING SENSE OF WORDS

Format:	Group/Syndicates
Type:	Communication practice/Icebreaker
Time:	15-20 minutes
Resources:	OHP, flip-chart, training resource ref: 33
Suitable for:	All levels

Purpose

A testing, thought-provoking and interesting activity to practise communication skills, styles and techniques.

Procedure

Distribute the OHP slide or list on a flip-chart. Ask delegates to

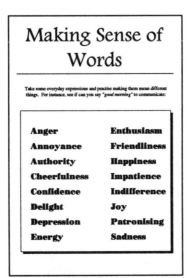

work in syndicates or invite volunteers to demonstrate to the group.

Ask delegates to think of a list of everyday expressions, such as:

'Good morning, it's a pleasure to meet you.'

'Yes, I had a very good holiday.'

'I wonder if I could take a few minutes to discuss some things with you.'

'I won't be able to make our meeting later on.'

Instruct delegates to practise one emotion or meaning in turn and experiment in saying each expression to have this tone or meaning. Don't be afraid to overact or exaggerate the purpose of the activity is to experiment and have fun.

An award will be given to the person who gives the most convincing and flexible communication.

After 10 or 15 minutes or when all the delegates have experimented in their groups, go round the room asking delegates to present their best examples to the group from the front of the room.

Allow delegates to vote on what they thought was the most convincing presentation.

Discussion Points

- ➲ What are the key behaviours to change?

- ➲ How easy was it to present 'false' emotions?

- ➲ How important is non-verbal communication such as body language and facial expression?

POINTS OF VIEW

Format:	*Individual*
Type:	*Session Starter/Icebreaker*
Time:	*45-60 minutes*
Resources:	*OHP, flip-chart, training resource ref: 34*
Suitable for:	*All levels*

Purpose

A testing, thought-provoking and interesting activity to practise presentation, persuasion and communication skills, styles and techniques.

Procedure

Distribute the handout, display as an OHP or draw on a flip-chart.

Ask delegates to work individually.

Make sure that everybody has a topic written down before continuing. Do this by going around the room and asking each delegate in turn to state their chosen subject. List these on a flip-chart for later reference.

Next, read out the following instructions, making sure that everybody is clear on what to do:

*'You will shortly have to give a three minute presentation stating the **opposite** point of view. For example, if you feel strongly against people who wear fur coats, you must speak for them!'*

An award will be given to the person who gives the most convincing and persuasive presentation.

Avoid entering any discussion about methods; simply repeat the instructions.

After 20 or 30 minutes or when all the delegates have prepared a brief presentation, go around the room asking delegates to present their case to the group from the front of the room. Remind them that they should aim to appear as committed and persuasive as possible.

Allow delegates to vote on what they thought was the most convincing presentation.

Discussion Points

- How did you approach designing a presentation on the opposite of a strongly held point of view?

- Was it easier than you expected or harder?

- What did you do (concisely) to appear more convincing?

- Which of the presentations were totally believable?

- Why or how could you tell if they were not believable?

- What are the key skills to 'sell' something that you don't believe?

- What should we be alert to in assessing honesty and integrity in others?

- When might this be useful?

GET IT OFF YOUR CHEST!

Format:	*Pairs/Syndicates*
Type:	*Self-disclosure/Icebreaker*
Time:	*15-20 minutes*
Resources:	*OHP, flip-chart, training resource ref: 35*
Suitable for:	*All levels*

Purpose

To exercise assertiveness and self-awareness.

Procedure

Distribute the handout or display on an OHP.

Ask delegates to work either in pairs or small syndicates.

Explain that an exercise will allow you (them) to express your true feelings about someone or something. Display the OHP slide.

Get It Off Your Chest!

Identify a specific authority figure in your life (paren
teacher, present or former boss) who has not treate
you as you would expect to be treated.
Choose a group member to play the role of this pers
and tell him or her how you are to be treated from
now on. **Demand specific changes in his or her
behaviour.** *The authority figure may respond.*

Read out the following instructions :

'Identify a specific authority figure in your life (parent, teacher, present or former boss) who has not treated you as you would expect to be treated.'

Choose a group member to play the role of this person and tell him or her how you are to be treated from now on. Demand specific changes in his or her behaviour.

The authority figure may respond.

Discussion Points

- How did you approach the conversation?
- What happened?
- Did you say what you wanted to say?
- What was the effect?
- How did the other person respond?
- How do you feel now?

HOW WELL DO YOU LISTEN?

Format:	*Individual*
Type:	*Communication skills*
Time:	*15-20 minutes*
Resources:	*Flip-chart, training resource ref: 36, 37*
Suitable for:	*All levels*

Purpose

To practise effective communication and interpersonal skills.

Procedure

Ask delegates to work individually.

Using a clear and deliberate voice, read out the passage of text on resource ref: 36 (or a similar one of your own).   Pause after punctuation but do not over-emphasise, speaking largely in a monotone. Delegates should not take any notes, but listen very carefully.

Continue with the test questions, asking delegates to write down their answers. When you have finished, repeat the questions once more.

Allow delegates a few minutes to finish writing down their answers.

After the time has elapsed, ask each delegate in turn to present their answers to the main group.

Run a short discussion around the points below, summarising by asking delegates to create a check-list to help them listen more attentively.

How Well Do You Listen?

Questions

Health and Safety At Work Act 1974

1. When was the Health and Safety At Work Act introduced?
2. Which two pieces of legislation did it replace?
3. What are the five main sections or areas it covers?
4. What size of companies are covered by the Act?
5. What must an employer display?
6. What is not considered an excuse for failing to provide safety equipment or standards?
7. What main requirements are placed on employees as a result of the Act?
8. How many working days were lost in 1994 through accident, job related illness or injury?
9. How many accidents occurred in the UK?
10. How many resulted in absences of 3 or more days?

Discussion Points

- How many answers did you get right?

- What were the things you were able to remember?

- How did you remember them?

- What stopped you from listening and retaining information?

Section 4: Personal Development

A Letter to Myself

Format:	Individual
Type:	End-of-course exercise
Time:	5-10 minutes
Resources:	Envelopes and stamps, training resource ref: 38
Suitable for:	All levels

Purpose

To improve and facilitate the transfer of ideas and skills from the training course to delegates' jobs and workplace.

Procedure

Ask delegates to work individually.

Distribute the handout.

Ask delegates to complete it and then hand it back to you, the trainer.

Optional: *You might choose to ask delegates to review their points while on the course. You may also choose to add your own comments to the letter before posting it.*

Collect the letters, place in envelopes and mail.

THIS IS ME!

Format:	*Pairs*
Type:	*Personal development/Communication*
Time:	*30-45 minutes*
Resources:	*Training resource ref: 39*
Suitable for:	*All levels*

Purpose

To change pace or act as a break between sessions. It is also a good introduction activity at the start of an event.

Procedure

Ask delegates to work in pairs.

This Is Me!

Working in pairs, please complete the following statements and the questions. Discuss your responses before moving on to the n question.

1. If I walked into a book shop and purchased a book for leisure reading, the title would probably be
2. If I stopped to listen to a "soap box" speaker, the subject of his her speech might be...
3. Reading the daily Newspaper, I notice an article that makes angry, it is probably about...
4. My favourite humorous T.V. show is ....   because? ....
5. Of the serious T.V. programmes I really
6. The last film I really enjoyed was ...
7. My favourite film of all time is probably
8. The last time I went to a party was did you enjoy it?
9. When I listen to the radio it is   (when and which station)
10. I belong to the following groups and associations...
11. People who know me best think I'm...
12. At a party or social gathering, my behaviour could best described as...
13. I would say my greatest communication strength is
14. I would say my greatest communication weakness is
15. Working with other people makes me
16. I relax by...
17. The one thing that I would like to change about myself
18. I prefer to work and spend time with people who ....

Distribute the handout.

Ask delegates to complete the statements and answer the questions, working through each question in pairs, and discuss their responses with each other before moving on to the next question.

Allow 20-30 minutes.

After all delegates have completed the questions, regain the group's attention and run a discussion on the following points.

Discussion Points

● What three adjectives best describe the other person you worked with, based on what you discovered about them during the exercise?

● Based on what you discovered during the exercise, what insights do you now have about each other?

● What can you learn from this exercise and apply to your own interpersonal skills?

COAT OF ARMS

Format:	*Individual/Group*
Type:	*Icebreaker/Session starter*
Time:	*45-50 minutes*
Resources:	*Flip-chart, training resource ref: 40*
Suitable for:	*All levels*

Purpose

To introduce delegates or to develop rapport further in a group context. Also to practise the skills of self-disclosure.

Procedure

Ask delegates to work individually.

Distribute the handout and ask delegates to complete and write down their answers to the seven questions on the worksheet.

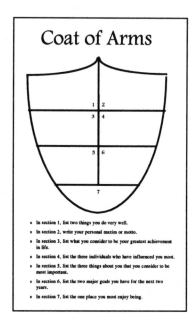

Allow 10-15 minutes.

Stress that delegates must not write their names on the sheet.

After the time has elapsed, distribute each worksheet so that no delegate receives their own, but they also do not know whose sheet they have.

Ask delegates to guess whose sheet they have, based on the answers given, and write this name on the top of the page.

Review answers with the group as a whole, discussing both why they identified a certain individual and perhaps the answers on the sheet themselves.

Discussion Points

● What clues were contained in the answers?

FIRST DAY AT WORK

Format:	*Syndicates*
Type:	*Improvement planning/Problem solving*
Time:	*30-40 minutes*
Resources:	*OHP, flip-chart, training resource ref: 41*
Suitable for:	*All levels*

Purpose

To generate ideas, discussion and share viewpoints on key issues.

Procedure

Introduce the exercise by highlighting that this is an excellent format for developing ideas, reinforcing learning points and encouraging self-analysis. It is also a very good way of accessing and sharing the knowledge, ideas and expertise of more experienced or successful salespeople with others in the group.

Write the trigger question on a flip-chart or OHP, or read it out to the group and ask them to write it down:

First Day at Work

What was your first full-time job?

Recall your first day in this job.

What advice would you give to someone just starting their first day at work?

What advice would you give to someone just starting their first day at work?

Break delegates into discussion groups of 4-8 people and ideally use different rooms. Allow 20-30 minutes to work.

A minimum of 20 minutes is normally required for discussion, with another 20-30 minutes for group summary presentations.

Set delegates the task of summarising the main points and considering these implications to themselves.

Ask each group to elect a spokesperson who can present the main points and allow each group about 10 minutes, with extra time for discussion as appropriate. Thank delegates for their contributions.

NB: Other suggested topics for discussion are listed overleaf.

PERSONAL STRENGTHS AND WEAKNESSES

Format:	Individual/Group
Type:	Climate changer/Icebreaker
Time:	30-40 minutes or as required
Resources:	Training resource ref: 42, 43
Suitable for:	All levels

Purpose

An exercise to develop and practise self-awareness, assertiveness and self-disclosure. It is also a useful team-building exercise.

Procedure

There are two handouts, 'Strengths' and 'Weaknesses'. It is perhaps best to use them at different times during a course.

Ask delegates to work individually to complete the worksheet, and then review their notes as part of a plenary group.

Either display as an OHP slide or distribute as a handout.

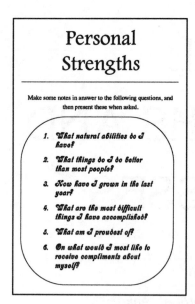

Personal Strengths

Make some notes in answer to the following questions, and then present these when asked.

1. What natural abilities do I have?
2. What things do I do better than most people?
3. How have I grown in the last year?
4. What are the most difficult things I have accomplished?
5. What am I proudest of?
6. On what would I most like to receive compliments about myself?

Personal Weaknesses

Make some notes in answer to the following questions, and then present these when asked.

1. What about me most upsets the people I work with?
2. What criticism would my closest friend give me if asked?
3. What am I least proud of?
4. What criticism would my boss give me?
5. What area(s) of my behaviour would I most like to improve?

Allow 5-10 minutes and then go around the group asking delegates to read out their notes.

Discussion Points

⮕ Was it harder or easier than you thought to be objective about your own personal characteristics?

⮕ How did you feel sharing personal information with group members?

SIX QUESTIONS TO CHANGE YOUR LIFE

Format:	*Individual/Group*
Type:	*Climate changer/Icebreaker*
Time:	*30-40 minutes or as required*
Resources:	*OHP, training resource ref: 44*
Suitable for:	*All levels*

Purpose

An exercise to develop and practise self-awareness, assertiveness and self-disclosure. It is also a useful team-building exercise and is valuable on any course involving goal setting, priority setting or time management.

Procedure

The handout lists six questions that refer us back to our core beliefs, values and motivations. They can be useful in gaining a perspective on our priorities and in renewing our direction and motivation. They also have the power to challenge our current direction.

The questions often uncover our comfort zones and the blocks that stop us striving for what we want. We realise that our barriers exist within us more than externally, and revolve around the fear of failure and the fear of rejection.

Ask delegates to work individually to complete the worksheet, and then review their notes as part of a group plenary.

Either display as an OHP slide or distribute as a handout. It is effective to reveal one question at a time on the OHP.

Six Questions

Please answer the following questions as quickly as possible, writing your first few, intuitive responses.

1. What would you do if you won £1million on the lottery next week?

2. What would you do if you only had six months to live?

3. What do you dream of achieving, attempting or experiencing?

4. What is your greatest fear that holds you back?

5. Describe your ideal job or working situation.

6. What one great thing would you dare to dream if you knew you couldn't fail?

Allow 10-15 minutes and then go around the group asking delegates to read out their notes. (NB: Some delegates may be unable to complete some questions, or will be reluctant to share their answers with the group.)

Discussion Points

➲ Was it harder or easier than you thought to be objective about your own personal characteristics?

➲ How did you feel sharing personal information with group members?

➲ What did you learn from each of the questions?

➲ Which question was harder to answer than others?

HOW ASSERTIVE ARE YOU?

Format:	Pairs/Group
Type:	Climate changer/Icebreaker
Time:	20-30 minutes or as required
Resources:	OHP, flip-chart, training resource ref: 45
Suitable for:	All levels

Purpose

An exercise to develop and practise self-awareness, assertiveness and self-disclosure, and also to become aware of levels of assertiveness.

Procedure

Ask delegates to work in pairs in discussing and completing the questions, and then review their notes as part of a plenary group.

Either display as an OHP slide or distribute as a handout.

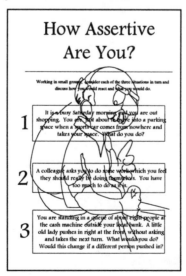

Allow 5-10 minutes and then go around the group asking delegates to read out their notes and lead a general discussion with the group as a whole.

Discussion Points

○ If you became aggressive how did this affect the situation? How did it affect you?

○ What would be the effect of doing or saying nothing? How would you feel?

○ What is the most appropriate response?

○ How would you define assertive behaviour? How is it different from aggressive behaviour?

HOW DO YOU SOLVE PROBLEMS?

Format:	Individual/Group
Type:	Climate changer/Icebreaker
Time:	30-40 minutes or as required
Resources:	OHP, training resource ref: 46
Suitable for:	All levels

Purpose

An exercise to develop and practise self-awareness with regard to problem solving.

Procedure

The handout lists five questions, which should help people gain an insight into their approach to problems, opportunities and challenges, these are:

1. *Can you give an example of one of the most difficult decisions that you ever had to make?*

2. *Can you give an example of a decision that was easy.*

3. *Can you give an example of a decision that turned out to be a mistake?*

4. *How do you weigh options when making BIG decisions.*

5. *What is your approach when making small everyday decisions, such as what to do at the weekend?*

These questions can be useful in gaining a better understanding of conscious and unconscious choices, and the way we approach decision making. These decisions can influence as well as be

---

influenced by our priorities, direction and motivation. They also have the power to challenge our current direction.

Ask delegates to work in pairs to discuss and complete the worksheet, and then review their notes as part of a plenary group.

Either display as an OHP slide or distribute as a handout.

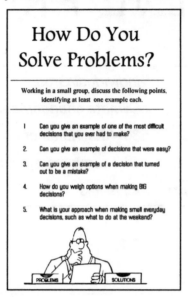

Allow 10-15 minutes and then go around the group asking delegates to read out their notes. (NB: Some delegates may be unable to complete some questions, or will be reluctant to share their answers with the group, be sensitive to this.)

Discussion Points

○ How do we make large decisions logic or intuition?

○ Do some choices seem really obvious? Others not so?

○ Are some decisions only fully understood in hindsight?

○ Are you aware of making conscious and unconscious decisions?

PRISONER'S DILEMMA

Format:	*Individual/Pairs*
Type:	*Climate changer/Icebreaker*
Time:	*5-10 minutes or as required*
Resources:	*OHP, flip-chart, training resource ref: 47*
Suitable for:	*All levels*

Purpose

A lively exercise to demonstrate our need to trust and work with others.

Procedure

Pair delegates off and arrange them so that each pair is facing each other across the room.

Distribute the handout or review on the OHP and make sure delegates are clear on the instructions.

Allow five minutes for delegates (without talking to others) to decide on their plea and write this secretly on a slip of paper.

Collect the slips and list responses on the flip-chart:

If both confess, both prisoners are automatically to be sentenced to ten years in jail and a million pound fine.

If only one confesses, that person will then be sentenced to community service and a million pound fine. The other person will then receive the jail term and fine.

If neither confesses, both will be convicted of complicity and sentenced to a five-year jail sentence and enforced bankruptcy.

Discussion Points

- ➲ Did you try to predict the other person's decision or choice?

- ➲ Did you try to anticipate what they thought you would do?

- ➲ How often do we make decisions based on assumptions of other people's actions and behaviours?

Section 5: Team Activities

Guess Who

Right to Strike

The Photocopy Machine

What Changes?

Signs of the Zodiac

Warm-up Game

Word Bluff

Three Things In Common

Challenge Match

Call in the Consultants

Wanted Poster

Brainstorm Exercise

Pirate Raid

Personal History

Precision Problem Solving

GUESS WHO

Format:	*Syndicates*
Type:	*Team building*
Time:	*15-20 minutes*
Resources:	OHP, *flip-chart, syndicate rooms, training resource ref: 48*
Suitable for:	*All levels*

Purpose

To introduce delegates to other group or team members in an informal and interesting way.

Procedure

Distribute the handout. (NB: The worksheet can also be distributed

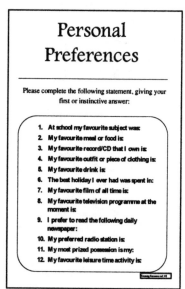

Personal Preferences

Please complete the following statement, giving your first or instinctive answer:

1. At school my favourite subject was:
2. My favourite meal or food is:
3. My favourite record/CD that I own is:
4. My favourite outfit or piece of clothing is:
5. My favourite drink is:
6. The best holiday I ever had was spent in:
7. My favourite film of all time is:
8. My favourite television programme at the moment is:
9. I prefer to read the following daily newspaper:
10. My preferred radio station is:
11. My most prized possession is my:
12. My favourite leisure time activity is:

before the course).

Ask delegates to take a few minutes to complete the statements, writing down their first or instinctive answers. **Do not explain the purpose or objective of this exercise at this stage.**

Ask delegates to work in syndicates or small groups, in separate rooms if possible, and to appoint a team leader or spokesperson.

The team leader then has to collect in the questionnaires, shuffle them and give out clues, one from each sheet, with the rest of the team trying to guess who the person is from the clues or responses given. (Alternatively, you can collect in all the questionnaires and run the exercise with the group as a whole.)

Allow 15-20 minutes, or until everybody has been identified.

After time has elapsed, ask each group in turn to present which responses gave people away, and which delegates were hardest to guess.

Run a discussion on the following points.

Discussion Points

○ How did you approach the group discussion?

○ What surprises did you find out about other people?

○ What responses made it difficult to guess whose answer it was?

RIGHT TO STRIKE

Format:	*Syndicates*
Type:	*Team building*
Time:	*30-45 minutes*
Resources:	*OHP, flip-chart, syndicate rooms, training resource ref: 49*
Suitable for:	*All levels*

Purpose

To establish the different views, values, ethics and beliefs in a group or team.

Procedure

Ask delegates to work in syndicates or small groups, in separate rooms if possible.

Distribute the handout.

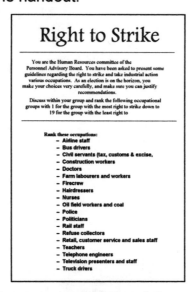

Ask delegates to complete it and then appoint a spokesperson to present their ranking and conclusions to the rest of the group.

Allow 15-20 minutes.

After the time has elapsed, ask each group in turn to present their summary.

Run a discussion on the following points.

Discussion Points

- How did you approach the group discussion?

- What method did you find effective?

- How accurately does the final ranking reflect the feeling and input of all group members?

- What sort of points emerged?

- What sort of team or leadership behaviours emerged?

- How did groups tolerate minority or extreme views?

- What can this teach us about working in teams?

THE PHOTOCOPY MACHINE

Format:	*Syndicates*
Type:	*Team building*
Time:	*30-45 minutes*
Resources:	*OHP, flip-chart, syndicate rooms, training resource ref: 50*
Suitable for:	*All levels*

Purpose

To establish the different views, values, ethics and beliefs in a group or team.

Procedure

Ask delegates to work in syndicates or small groups, in separate rooms if possible.

Distribute the handout.

The Photocopy Machine

"The photocopy machine broke down in your office this morning and has only just been repaired. It is now 4:00 PM and by 8:30am tomorrow, 150 folders have to be filled with 20 pages of material for a conference. It is your job as a manager to tell your assistant that he or she must stay late and do all the photocopying. You happen to know that your subordinate has tickets for a popular concert tonight, for which he or she stood in line for hours and to which they have been looking forward for weeks."

Discussion Points

● How did you approach the discussions

WHAT CHANGES?

Format:	*Syndicates of 5-7 people*
Type:	*Icebreaker/Session starter*
Time:	*15-20 minutes*
Resources:	*Reading material, such as newspaper etc.*
Suitable for:	*All levels*

Purpose

To practise communication, listening and concentration skills.

Procedure

Ask delegates to work in groups of 5-7 people, seated in a circle.

One person has to start by reading aloud from a book or newspaper, **and must keep reading until the end of the passage**.

Instruct the person on the right to repeat every word they hear to the person on their right, **as they hear it**.

This person must now repeat exactly what they have to the person on their right, **as they hear it**.

Continue until the last person finishes talking.

Run a short discussion on the following points.

Discussion Points

● What changes were made to the passage read aloud?

● Why?

● What stopped you from concentrating?

SIGNS OF THE ZODIAC

Format:	Syndicates of 5-7 people
Type:	Icebreaker/Session starter
Time:	15-20 minutes
Resources:	Flip-chart
Suitable for:	All levels

Purpose

To introduce delegates to others in a group in a fun and trivial manner.

Procedure

Ask delegates if there are any Leos here today.

Write their names on the flip-chart with their star sign against it.

Continue with each star sign.

Ask members with the various star signs to sit together and discuss if there are any similarities. If there are any star signs with only one representative, ask that person to join another group.

Allow 5 minutes.

Run a short discussion on the following points.

Discussion Points

- Are there any similarities or common traits?

- Can you guess a person's star sign by their personality?

WARM-UP GAME

Format:	Group/Syndicates
Type:	Icebreaker/Session starter
Time:	20-30 minutes
Resources:	OHP, flip-chart, large training room, training resource ref: 51
Suitable for:	All levels

Purpose

This is a good exercise to run at the start of any event. It might be described as a meta-exercise, an icebreaker activity that designs an exercise as part of its main function. It is particularly suitable for large groups of up to about 30 delegates.

Procedure

Form delegates into syndicates of 5-6 people, give each group a name or reference and ask each to elect a team leader.

Display the OHP slide and read the instructions:

'Take 5-10 minutes to design a 5-10 minute warm-up exercise that you can run in 5-10 minutes' time.'

Warm-up Game

TAKE 5-10 MINUTES TO DESIGN A 5-10 MINUTE WARM-UP EXERCISE THAT YOU CAN RUN IN 5-10 MINUTES' TIME.

STAFF PICNIC

Allow 5-10 minutes and encourage delegates to work quickly. Avoid becoming involved in any questions or debates. Delegates can use any resources found in the training room.

After 5 minutes or so, call out the name of each group in turn and ask each spokesperson to tell the group what happened and outline their exercise if they have indeed completed one. (Select one or more and run them later in the course.)

Run a short discussion on the following points.

Discussion Points

● What happened in your team?

● How did you structure the discussion?

● How did the team work together?

● If you failed to arrive at a solution what could you learn from your approach?

● What role did the leader take?

WORD BLUFF

Format:	Syndicates
Type:	Climate changer/Energiser
Time:	15-20 minutes or as required
Resources:	OHP, flip-chart, training resources ref: 52-62
Suitable for:	All levels

Purpose

To practise creative communication, team work and presentation skills(the ability to bluff!).

Procedure

On each of the handouts/OHP slides is a set of word definitions, only one of which is correct.

The purpose of the exercise is to 'bluff' the other team or audience into believing that an incorrect meaning, rather than the real meaning of the word, is correct. It makes an excellent addition to any training course, presentation or group event.

Select two or three people, or two teams of three, with the rest of the group acting as the scoring audience.

Distribute handouts and give teams a few minutes to decide who is going to present each of the three definitions.

NB: None of the handouts has the answers on, so delegates must *assume* that each one could be true. You could, alternatively, let teams in on the secret.

Run the first round:

Each team takes it in turns to present their word (write this on the flip-chart) and their three proposed definitions They must make the two false meanings sound as believable as possible.

After all three versions have been presented, the other teams or audience vote for the definition they believe to be correct. The one with the most votes is taken as the consensus.

or not and score two points for choosing the right definition, or falling for a bluff, and lose two points if they are unsuccessful.

Other rounds can then be played either later during the course, or as part of a full competition of, say, three or four rounds.

The team with the most points wins. In the event of a tie, the team with the greatest style wins.

Discussion Points

○ How were you able to detect the real definitions?

○ Are some people better at bluffing than others?

○ Does the word being defined make a difference?

○ How do you bluff successfully?

Answers

▢ *Word Bluff/1 - definition 1 is true*

Dieldrin is a crystalline substance, consisting of a chlorinated derivative of naphthalene; a contact insecticide.

▢ *Word Bluff/2 - definition 1 is true*

The pseudepigrapha are various Jewish writings from the first century B.C. to the first century A.D. that claim to have been divinely revealed but have been excluded from the Old Testament.

▢ *Word Bluff/3 - definition 3 is true*

Damask is a reversible fabric, usually silk or linen, with a pattern woven into it. It is used for table linen, curtains etc.

▢ *Word Bluff/4 - definition 2 is true*

A riffle is a contrivance on the bottom of a sluice, containing grooves for trapping particles of gold (as in mining).

▢ *Word Bluff/5 - definition 1 is true*

A defoliant is a chemical sprayed or dusted on trees to cause their leaves to fall.

☐ *Word Bluff/6 - definition 3 is true*

Scleroderma is a chronic disease common among women, characterised by thickening and hardening of the skin.

☐ *Word Bluff/7 - definition 2 is true*

Torticollis is an abnormal position of the head, which is usually characterised by the bent position of the neck to one side.

☐ *Word Bluff/8 - definition 1 is true*

Monetarism is the theory that inflation is caused by an excess quantity of money in an economy.

☐ *Word Bluff/9 - definition 3 is true*

Geodesy is the branch of science concerned with determining the exact positioning of geographical points, and the shape and size of the earth.

☐ *Word Bluff/10 - definition 1 is true*

A trireme is an ancient Greek galley with three banks of oars on each side.

THREE THINGS IN COMMON

Format:	*Pairs*
Type:	*Sessions starter*
Time:	*5-10 minutes*
Resources:	*OHP, flip-chart, training resource ref: 63*
Suitable for:	*All levels*

Purpose

To allow delegates to get to know each other and their backgrounds at the beginning of a course or meeting. This exercise is also a good way of practising rapport-building skills.

Procedure

Ask delegates to stand up, circulate around the room and introduce themselves to other delegates, ideally those they have not met before, and find at least three other people that they have something in common with. Allow about 5-10 minutes.

After this time, ask delegates to return to their seats and go around the room asking each delegate to say what they were able to identify in common with the other person. In a larger group, do this for about ten or so delegates, or until themes begin to repeat themselves.

Three Things In Common

Circulate around the room and introduce yourself to other delegates, ideally someone you have not met before, and find at least three other people that you have things in common with.

Discussion Points

- How easy was it to find things in common?

- What type of questions did you ask?

- Is this exercise effective in building rapport and empathy?

- How do you feel towards people who only ten minutes ago were (perhaps) total strangers?

- What questions would you ask if you did the exercise again?

CHALLENGE MATCH

Format:	*Syndicates*
Type:	*Energiser*
Time:	*20-30 minutes*
Resources:	*Flip-chart, syndicate room, training resource ref: 64*
Suitable for:	*All levels*

Purpose

To review course content and test key learning points in a fun and active manner with delegates working in teams.

Procedure

Form delegates into two teams or syndicates.

Distribute handout, or display as an OHP slide.

Challenge Match

Based on everything we have discussed or covered in the previous training course or session, prepare eight challenging questions to ask the other team. Just for the fun of it, add two additional questions about anything at all which have nothing to do with this course. Teams will exchange questions alternately, and you will earn two points for a correct answer, and one bonus point for every incorrect answer by the other team.

Your eight questions:

1.

2.

3.

4.

5.

6.

7.

8.

Read out and review the instructions with delegates, making sure that everyone is clear on what they have to do.

'Based on everything we have discussed or covered in the previous training course or session, prepare eight challenging questions to ask the other team.'

NB: A version of this activity can be run based on company history or information, product knowledge or some other related topic.

'Just for the fun of it, add two additional questions about anything at all which have nothing to do with this course.

Teams will exchange questions alternately, and you will earn two points for a correct answer, and one bonus point for every incorrect answer by the other team."

Set a time limit of ten minutes for the creation of questions.

After the time limit reassemble teams, facing each other, and run a 'quiz show' format, keeping score on the flip-chart. Award two points for each correct answer and one bonus point to the other team for an incorrect answer.

CALL IN THE CONSULTANTS

Format:	*Pairs/Triads*
Type:	*Problem solving*
Time:	*40-60 minutes*
Resources:	*OHP, flip-chart, training resource ref: 65*
Suitable for:	*All levels*

Purpose

For delegates to practise their problem-solving ability around the theme of the course and to reach their own conclusions about ways of improving in any particular area.

Procedure

Divide the group into teams of 3-5, and ask each team to give themselves a name, perhaps the name of a rather grand-sounding consultancy company.

Distribute the handout.

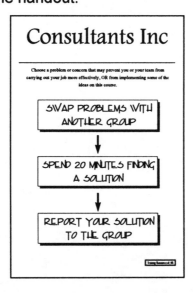

Ask delegates to choose a question, problem or concern that may prevent them or their team from carrying out their job more effectively.

Alternatively, you might focus assignments on 'How to implement some of the ideas on this course'.

Set a time limit (15-20 minutes), and ask delegates to write that problem on a card or piece of paper. Try and be as specific as possible.

Allow 30 minutes.

After 20 minutes, or when everybody has finished, collect in all the problems or questions and redistribute them to different groups.

Instruct the groups that they now have to find a solution to the problem or question.

Allow about 20-30 minutes.

After 20 minutes, or when all groups have finished, ask each group to present their solution to the other groups, explaining the reasoning behind their proposal.

Discussion Points

➲ Is it easier to be objective or creative when it is not your problem?

➲ Did working in a group provide a better or quicker solution?

➲ Do others have similar problems to you?

WANTED POSTER

Format:	Pairs/Triads
Type:	Review of key personal skills
Time:	30 minutes
Resources:	OHP, flip-chart, training resource ref: 66

Purpose

This exercise is a really good activity to raise the energy level on a course. It also is a good way to summarise key points from a course or meeting.

Procedure

This activity gets everybody up, talking and moving around the room. It is also impossible to take it too seriously, although the content of the discussion and posters reinforces some key attributes needed for success in their profession or organisation.

Introduce the exercise by asking delegates to recall seeing old Hollywood cowboy movies where the sheriff would ride into town and pin-up a WANTED! poster at the beginning.

Well, the people WANTED! in this company are good people!

Next divide delegates into groups of 2-3 and hand them several sheets of flip-chart paper each. Show the OHP.

Wanted Poster

TASK.

You have to design a "Wanted Poster" for a company superstar for your job.
The poster should describe how people would recognise this person what they would look like, where they might be last seen, and explain just what sort of character he or she is.
It should also say that a large reward is available for anybody helping to find this person.

Tell them they have to design a 'Wanted Poster' for a 'superstar'.

The poster should describe how people would recognise this person, what they would look like, where they might be last seen, and explain just what sort of character he or she is.

It should also say that a large reward is available for anybody helping to find this person.

Allow about 15-20 minutes

Pin the posters around the room and refer to them as you wish to draw attention to key points during the training course or meeting.

BRAINSTORM EXERCISE

Format:	*Syndicates*
Type:	*Team building/Problem solving*
Time:	*30-40 minutes*
Resources:	*OHP, flip-chart, training resources ref: 67, 68*
Suitable for:	*All levels*

Purpose

This is an expanded discussion group, allowing a much more free and open exchange of ideas and possibilities.

Procedure

Explain that the objective of this exercise is to generate practical ideas, discussion and specific measures on how to implement improvements to your organisation or key issues, **write this on the flip-chart or on the handout.**

Next, form delegates into groups of 4-8 people, and arm each with a flip-chart (or flip-chart pad). A separate room or area is required for each group.

Ask each group to agree a 'note taker' and a 'facilitator'. The task of the note taker is to write down **all** ideas and suggestions that arise, without judgement, no matter how ridiculous. The facilitator's job is to encourage as much participation and as many ideas as possible, **not** to judge or control the discussion, but to encourage discussion.

Next, explain that each group should first spend time generating as many ideas as possible (show the OHP slide), and then rank each idea and produce a short list of their best proposals. (If desired, this exercise can often be allowed to run for longer.)

Brainstorming

To get a few good ideas...

...first generate lots of ideas!

After about 25-30 minutes, reassemble the group and ask each syndicate group to review their list and present their short list of the 'best few'. List these on a flip-chart or OHP slide.

Finally, ask delegates to make a note of any actions based on these good ideas.

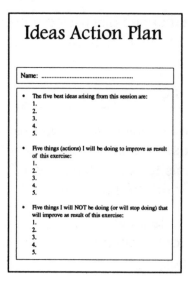

Ideas Action Plan

Name: ....

- The five best ideas arising from this session are:
  1.
  2.
  3.
  4.
  5.

- Five things (actions) I will be doing to improve as result of this exercise:
  1.
  2.
  3.
  4.
  5.

- Five things I will NOT be doing (or will stop doing) that will improve as result of this exercise:
  1.
  2.
  3.
  4.
  5.

Discussion Points

➦ How is it to be creative and think laterally?

➦ Did it help to work in a group?

➦ Was the process enjoyable?

➦ Did it produce some good ideas?

PIRATE RAID

Format:	*Teams*
Type:	*Session starter/Introduction*
Time:	*20-30 minutes*
Resources:	*A bit of nerve! Training resources ref: 69, 70*

Purpose

A good warm-up and ice-breaking exercise, particularly for longer courses, which tests delegates' persuasion, creativity and lateral thinking skills, as well as a sense of team working.

Procedure

This activity asks delegates to 'raid' and 'plunder' the training venue, or nearby shops etc., to obtain a list of items. It doesn't matter if some of the items are unobtainable, or cannot be obtained in the time limit: this is part of the fun. This activity, if run at the beginning of a course, will get delegates working together, and should show you a little about some of the personalities. It might be prudent to make sure that all items are returned, and if using a hotel just check with the duty manager before, and perhaps after, the exercise that there are no problems.

Form delegates into two teams and distribute the handouts, one to each team. Allow 15-20 minutes.

Pirate Raid - Team A

As a test of your powers of persuasion, creativity and lateral thinking, collect as many of the items listed in 15 minutes or less. One point will be awarded for every item collected, and one bonus point for every minute under 15 minutes, but only if all items are collected.

- ✓ some foreign currency
- ✓ cheque for £1 million
- ✓ a boiled sweet
- ✓ the name and address of a complete stranger (in their handwriting)
- ✓ a piece of underwear
- ✓ a cooking utensil
- ✓ the price of a Ford Escort
- ✓ a car number plate
- ✓ a toilet roll
- ✓ a coin dated before 1980
- ✓ a £50 note
- ✓ the telephone number of the British Embassy in Paris
- ✓ the full name and date of birth of your managing director

---

Pirate Raid - Team B

As a test of your powers of persuasion, creativity and lateral thinking, collect as many of the items listed in 15 minutes or less. One point will be awarded for every item collected, and one bonus point for every minute under 15 minutes, but only if all items are collected.

- ✓ some foreign currency
- ✓ cheque for a £1 million
- ✓ a piece of fruit
- ✓ the name and address of a complete stranger (in their handwriting)
- ✓ a flower
- ✓ a workshop tool
- ✓ the price of a dozen eggs
- ✓ a sign or notice
- ✓ a very old newspaper or magazine
- ✓ a coin dated before 1980
- ✓ a £50 note
- ✓ the telephone number of the French Embassy in London
- ✓ the full name and date of birth of your youngest employee

Allow 15-20 minutes for the 'pirate raid' and a further 5-10 minutes to see which team has won, and to discuss how various items were obtained.

(And make sure that any items 'borrowed' are returned!)

PERSONAL HISTORY

Format:	*Teams/Syndicates*
Type:	*Icebreaker/Session starter*
Time:	*20-30 minutes*
Resources:	*Training resource ref: 71*
Suitable for:	*All levels*

Purpose

To allow delegates to get to know each other and their backgrounds at the beginning of a course or meeting.

Procedure

Form delegates into groups or syndicates and ask them to find out some personal facts (where they live, age, family, etc) about their colleagues, and also the answer to the following question.

'What are the highlights in your career?'

Distribute the handouts.

This should take about 15 minutes.

Reform the group and ask each syndicate to elect a spokesperson in turn to present a brief summary of their group, making it as interesting and relevant as possible.

You might like to add your own introduction at the end.

Conclude the exercise by running a short group discussion around the following themes, making a note of key points that arise on a flip-chart or OHP.

Discussion Points

○ How many people started their careers in another profession and moved into this one?

○ How many people started work with a completely different company or with different products or services?

○ How were you able to transfer your skills across?

PRECISION PROBLEM SOLVING

Format:	*Syndicates*
Type:	*Climate changer/Energiser*
Time:	*30 minutes or as required*
Resources:	*OHP, flip-chart, training resources ref: 72, 73, 74*
Suitable for:	*All levels*

Purpose

To get delegates working in teams and practise problem-solving and thinking skills.

Procedure

Introduce the exercise by asking the group to answer the following puzzle:

> *'If three days ago was the day before Monday, what will the day after tomorrow be?'*

Wait for answers to offered, and keep going until the correct answer is arrived at. *(The answer is Friday, see below.)*

Continue by highlighting that the first step towards solving any problem is to decide what the problem, or question, is in the first place.

When you form an idea of what you are looking for, you have a goal for your thinking and you have a place to start. In the first puzzle, the objective is to find out what the day after tomorrow will be. With this in mind, you can restate the puzzle in simpler terms:

The day before Monday is Sunday. If three days ago was Sunday, then today is Wednesday. If today is Wednesday, then the day after tomorrow is Friday. The puzzle becomes almost trivial when you arrange the information clearly.

Ask delegates to work in syndicates (groups of 3-4) on this exercise, which will test their problem-solving and thinking skills.

Next, set the task, by distributing the handout or displaying as an OHP slide. (Use one or more.)

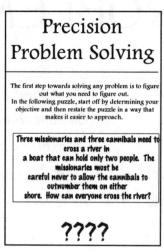

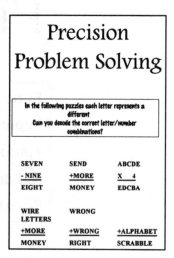

Allow about 15 minutes and then go around the group asking delegates to read out their solutions for each problem.

Discussion Points

➲ How did you go about solving each situation?

➲ What techniques were effective?

➲ Is there a pattern that you can notice?

Answers:

Tallahassee Zoo

If (Beasts + Birds is 30) then (Beasts is 30 - Birds). Into the equation (4 x Beasts + 2 x Birds is 100) substitute (Beasts is 30 - Birds) giving 4 x (30 -Birds) + (2 x Birds) is 100. Therefore 120 - (4 x Birds) + (2 x Birds) is 100. 120 - 2 x Birds is 100. 20 is 2 x Birds. There are ten birds and twenty beasts in the zoo.

Three Missionaries and Three Cannibals

First a missionary and a cannibal cross. The missionary returns. Two cannibals cross. One cannibal returns. Two missionaries cross. A missionary and a cannibal return. Two missionaries cross. One cannibal returns. Two cannibals cross. One cannibal returns. The remaining two cannibals cross.

Word Additions

Seven - nine - eight. There are two solutions

21514 - 4641   16873

54146 - 6764   47382

Send more money

9567 + 1085   10652

ABCDE x 4 - EDCBA

21978 x 4   87912

Wire more money

9762 + 1062   10824

Wrong + Wrong - Right

25938 + 25938   51876

Letters + Alphabet - Scrabble

7088062 + 17531908   24619970

Section 6: Creative Thinking

RORSCHACH
INKBLOT

Format:	*Individual*
Type:	*Icebreaker/Session starter*
Time:	*10-15 minutes*
Resources:	*OHP, flip-chart, training resource ref: 75*
Suitable for:	*All levels*

Purpose

To show how we shape our perception of the world by what we 'choose' to see or the meaning we put on things and events.

Procedure

Ask delegates to work individually.

Display the OHP slide or distribute as a handout.

Allow 5 minutes, encourage delegates to work quietly and quickly and make notes on the shapes and images that they can see. Avoid becoming involved in any questions or debates.

After 5 minutes, go around the room asking delegates to say what they think they have found.

Run a short discussion on the following points.

Discussion Points

- How many shapes did people see?

- Did anybody find things that nobody else did?

- Can you see the shapes and images once others have found them first?

- What can this tell us about how we view the world, events and problems?

THE BIG WIN!

Format:	*Individual/Group*
Type:	*Icebreaker/Session starter*
Time:	*20-30 minutes*
Resources:	*Flip-chart*
Suitable for:	*All levels*

Purpose

This is a good exercise to run at the start of any event, particularly at a time-management course. In a general sense it can encourage delegates to make the most of their time in the training course, and obviously relates to good time-management attitudes.

Procedure

Write £86,400 in large text on the flip-chart.

Describe how the group has just won a large prize in the National Lottery as part of a syndicate. The individual prize money is **£86,400 each**. Working in pairs, decide how you are going to spend your money, as well as persuading your colleague on what he or she should buy. Under the agreed rules of the syndicate, any money left unspent by the end of the day gets distributed among the other members.

Allow 3-4 minutes, encourage delegates to work quickly.

When all delegates have finished, compare responses on the flip-chart and run a short discussion on the most popular or differing items.

Ask delegates if they notice anything significant about the amount of £86,400.

In fact, 86,400 is exactly the same number of seconds that we are given at the start of every day.

Discussion Points

- If we don't decide how to spend our time, who does?

- If we waste our time, what happens to it?

- Do we ever plan our time as carefully or as thoughtfully as we spent an imaginary £86,400?

- Is time more valuable than money?

- What would you do if you had more time?

LIFE METAPHORS

Format:	Individual
Type:	Creative thinking
Time:	15-20 minutes
Resources:	Flip-chart, training resource ref: 76
Suitable for:	Managers, professionals, executives

Purpose

To give a different perspective on how we view our careers, and therefore lives, and also to identify and examine underlying metaphors that affect our thinking and perception.

Procedure

Ask delegates to work individually, and be ready to share their ideas in the group discussion that will follow.

Distribute the handout, or display as a slide.

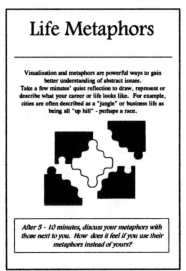

Life Metaphors

Visualisation and metaphors are powerful ways to gain better understanding of abstract issues.
Take a few minutes' quiet reflection to draw, represent or describe what your career or life looks like. For example, cities are often described as a "jungle" or business life as being all "up hill" - perhaps a race.

After 5 - 10 minutes, discuss your metaphors with those next to you. How does it feel if you use their metaphors instead of yours?

Introduce the activity by saying that visualisation and metaphors are powerful ways to gain better understanding of abstract issues. They also shape our perception and thinking. For example, 'concrete jungle', 'time is money', 'it's an uphill struggle', 'price war'.

Read out and review the instructions with delegates, making sure that everyone is clear on what to do.

'Take a few minutes of quiet reflection to draw, represent or describe how your career or life looks . For example, cities are often described as a "jungle" or business life as being all "up hill", perhaps a race.'

After 5-10 minutes, ask people to discuss their metaphors with those next to them. Open up a group discussion, allowing people to share their drawings and observations.

Discussion Points

➲ Are there any recurring themes or metaphors?

➲ How does it feel if you use their metaphors instead of yours?

➲ Did anyone think of their career as a journey or a river? These are common examples.

➲ Did anyone associate with animals or figures, with butterflies, eagles, warriors?

MENTAL TOUR

Format:	*Group*
Type:	*Climate setter*
Time:	*5-10 minutes*
Resources:	*Silence! Training resources ref: 77, 78*
Suitable for:	*All levels*

Purpose

To change the pace of a training session and allow delegates to practise visualisation and relaxation techniques.

Procedure

Introduce the exercise by explaining that creative visualisation is a valuable skill in many areas of our lives. For example, rehearsing situations in advance, problem solving and setting goals.

Ask the delegates to sit in as relaxed a way as possible and close their eyes.

♪ ♫ *Note: You may choose to play some relaxing classical or similar music as a background to this exercise.*

Speaking slowly and deliberately, read the passage of your choice. Pause at the end and wait for delegates' attention to return naturally.

Mental Tour -
The Orange

Imagine that you're holding an orange.
Picture what it would feel like,
what it would look like, try to form as clear an image as
you can. Now imagine peeling off the skin,
pulling apart the segments,
and biting into a piece.

After a moment, examine a segment very closely.
Ask yourself what the orange would look like
if you could enlarge it a thousand times, or a million
times.
What might the cells look like?
What might the molecules look like?

For the next couple of minutes,
try to become aware of everything
that you know and don't know about oranges.

Think about what makes an orange an orange,
why it tastes the way it does,
how many types of oranges there may be,
how oranges may have evolved through time,
what purposes oranges may serve,
and how to make a good orange marmalade.
As you think about the orange,
pay close attention to the quality of your thoughts.

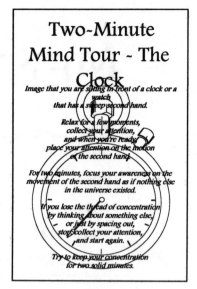

Two-Minute
Mind Tour - The
Clock

Image that you are sitting in front of a clock or a
watch
that has a sweep second hand.

Relax for a few moments,
collect your attention,
and when you're ready
place your attention on the motion
of the second hand.

For two minutes, focus your awareness on the
movement of the second hand as if nothing else
in the universe existed.

If you lose the thread of concentration
by thinking about something else,
or just by spacing out,
stop, collect your attention,
and start again.

Try to keep your concentration
for two solid minutes.

There are two sample passages -'Orange' and 'The Clock' - or you may well be able to create your own. For example, describe the sensation of lying on a beach.

You can vary the clock exercise by asking delegates to focus on a clock in the room.

Discussion Points

- ➥ Orange example: did you find yourself swallowing as if you were eating an orange?

- ➥ How vivid was your image?

- ➥ How much detail did you manage to generate?

- ➥ Did your brain give you any unexpected or unusual images or thoughts?

- ➥ What other sensations did you notice?

METATTENTION

Format:	*Individual/Group*
Type:	*Session starter*
Time:	*5-10 minutes*
Resources:	*None, training resource ref: 79*
Suitable for:	*All levels*

Purpose

To demonstrate that the world is how we see it, not what it is. Or, 'the map is not the territory'; as the expression goes.

Procedure

Introduce the exercise with the following questions and thoughts:

Task: List five recent television commercials that you recall easily. What are the topics?

Next time you browse through a magazine or newspaper, be aware of what you notice.

Notice what adverts, articles and pages your eye is drawn towards.

What does it feel like to have your attention diverted to something?

What part of your mind is controlling your attention?

Display the OHP or simply read out the instructions.

Look around the room and find six objects that contain circles.

Metattention

Look around the room and find six objects that contain circles.

With circle awareness, you'll find circles jumping out all around you - the top of a cup, the end of a pencil, the face of a screw in a light switch.

When you set your attention to look for something, you almost always find it. You just need to know what you're looking for.

Discussion Points

- What do you pay attention to which determines what your world is like.

- Focus on problems, and your world is full of obstacles.

- Focus on nothing in particular, and your world is a clutter of unrelated experiences.

- Focus on creative ideas, and your world opens to a realm of unlimited possibilities.

- People find what they are looking for. Is this true?

- Discuss and identify examples of people finding what they are looking for.

VISUALISATION

Format:	Pairs
Type:	Session starter
Time:	15-20 minutes
Resources:	OHP, flip-chart, training resources ref: 80, 81, 82
Suitable for:	All levels

Purpose

To practise the skill of visualisation and imaging.

Procedure

Introduce the exercise by describing the extraordinary skill of Nicolas Tesla, the inventor of the fluorescent light bulb, the AC generator and high-voltage electricity. He had an extraordinary capacity to create vivid imagery. He routinely envisaged three-dimensional images of complicated machines. These were complete in every detail and as clear as blueprints. Even more astonishingly, Tesla tested his machines mentally by letting them run in his mind for several weeks and thoroughly examining their components for signs of wear.

Tesla was probably an 'eidetic' imager: his mental pictures were as bright and clear as his eyesight. An eidetic imager, a person who has a truly photographic memory, can look at the front page of a newspaper for a few seconds, turn away, and then read the entire page in his or her mind. For an eidetic imager, mental pictures are remarkably accurate and long lasting.

Almost a century ago, psychologist Francis Galton devised a questionnaire that probed the clarity of people's imaginations. Besides discovering that few people are true eidetic imagers, Galton discovered that people's visualisation skills do not improve easily. Here is a modification of his test.

Distribute the handout and ask delegates to perform the exercise by quiet reflection.

Visualisation/1

Almost a century ago, psychologist Francis Galton devised a questionnaire that probed the clarity of people's imaginations. Besides discovering that few people are true eidetic imagers, Galton discovered that people's visualisation skills do not improve easily. Here is a modification of his test.

Visualisation/2

Imagine last night's dinner. Spend a minute or two picturing the scene. Visualise the people you were with, the surroundings, the table settings, the taste of the food, the sounds you heard. Before reading on, take some time to allow your image to build, piece by piece.

START NOW.

Visualisation/3

Answer the following questions about your image.

- ✓ Is your image clear or indistinct?
- ✓ Is the image brighter or dimmer than the original scene?
- ✓ Are all parts of the scene sharply defined at the same instant, or are some parts clearer than others?
- ✓ Does the image appear in colour or in shades of grey?
- ✓ Can you form a single visual image of the entire dining room?
- ✓ Can you retain a steady image of your dinner plate? If so, does it grow brighter?
- ✓ Can you mentally see your dinner plate, your hands holding a knife and fork, a person's face sitting across from you all at the same time?
- ✓ Can you feel the texture of the food?
- ✓ Can you picture what people were wearing?

Discussion Point

How did you do with the exercise? If you are like most people you probably found that there are places in your imagery that are rich and vibrant, and places that are less clear. Perhaps you could imagine the people's faces, but not the shape of the cups. Maybe you could recreate the smell of the food but not the taste, or recreate the acoustics of the room but not recall the shape of the cutlery. Perhaps all you could generate was the idea of yesterday's dinner without actually seeing any image at all.

Visualisation - Extra Trainer's Notes

Regardless of how vividly mental pictures appear, our imagery tends to be far less accurate than we imagine it is. Draw a pound coin, or your front door, or a telephone dial's digits and letters, or your car's dashboard, things you see every day, and you'll find gaps and holes in your mental images.

The accuracy of a mental image depends greatly on how much you have analysed the original object. If you've never really examined a pound coin closely, you probably won't be able to form an accurate image of it. If you rarely give your dashboard a second glance, you won't have more than an abstract sense of what it looks like.

To add life to imagery, you need to side-step verbal thinking and use your graphic analysis muscles.

When you want to form a clear image, recall the key elements gleaned from your analysis, the sense of proportion and the arrangements of component shapes. Allow the image to appear in front of you. It may be difficult at first, if you do not have the habit of visualising, but if you give yourself time the images will grow brighter and steadier.

What objects can you practise visualising? Faces, clothes, cars, buildings, company logos, patterns on concrete, pens, pencils, wallpaper designs, book covers or anything that catches your interest is fair game. Besides encouraging you to pay more attention to your environment, visualising everyday objects gives you a deeper appreciation of what's happening around you and deepens your sense of reality.

When you read a novel, take an extra moment to picture the events. Visualise the setting, the characters and the action. Choose a specific spatial viewpoint and let the story unfold in front of you. Similarly, next time you read a newspaper article, visualise what's happening in the article. If you read about a political leader making a statement, picture the politician speaking the words. If you read about an earthquake, imagine what it would feel like to be there. You'll be astonished at how much more you will remember of what you have read.

As you practise visualisation, you may find that at times images appear slowly, as in a jigsaw puzzle, building up piece by piece. At other times images emerge all at once, spontaneously in full living colour, giving you a taste of how brightly and clearly mental pictures may appear to an eidetic imager. More than anything else, the practice of forming sharp, accurate mental images encourages you to really see, remember and visualise.

GOAL VISUALISATION

Format:	Pairs
Type:	Session starter/climate changer
Time:	25-30 minutes
Resources:	OHP, flip-chart, training resource ref: 83
Suitable for:	All levels

Purpose

To allow delegates to practise the skills of visualising key skills and behaviours, goals and ambitions. It can be linked to the topic or skills being presented in the course.

Procedure

Ask delegates to work individually and be ready to contribute their results to the group discussion that will follow.

Next ask delegates to select a specific goal or behaviour. Distribute the handout or display the OHP slide.

Once a goal or new behaviour has been selected, it is vital to form a vivid mental picture of yourself doing or having something that you want to do, or have.

In this visualisation, three things are important: first, include details by engaging all of your senses; second, imagine yourself enjoying the scenario you wish for yourself: and third, picture the scene happening on a specific date. By encouraging you to focus on your objectives this visualisation helps to stir up your motivation. Start with a small, easy-to-reach goal and work up to larger more encompassing goals.

Ask delegates to make detailed notes on these images.

After 10-15 minutes go around the room and ask each delegate to share their images and goals.

Discussion Points

➲ Did the images and scenes begin to 'flow' after you had focused on a goal?

➲ How much detail were you able to generate?

➲ Have you used this technique in the past?

PERSONAL PERFORMANCE REHEARSAL

Format:	*Individual/Group review*
Type:	*Session starter/Climate changer*
Time:	*25-30 minutes*
Resources:	*OHP, flip-chart, training resource ref: 84*
Suitable for:	*All levels*

Purpose

To allow delegates to practise mental rehearsal techniques for a forthcoming presentation.

Procedure

Ask delegates to work individually and be ready to contribute their results to the group discussion that will follow.

Next ask delegates to select a forthcoming presentation. Distribute the handout or display the OHP slide.

Goal Visualisation

1. Select your forthcoming presentation:

If you are going to give a presentation - in a sales meeting, in a speech, or in an interview - picture a range of possible scenarios. Begin with an ideal outcome.

Imagine you're performing in top shape with things happening exactly as you want them to. Then picture a mediocre outcome, with things happening close to the ideal but not quite. Then visualise the worst possible outcome with you stumbling over yourself. In the process of rehearsing these scenarios, you prepare yourself for mishaps and problems. Then once you have worked through the possibilities, focus on the ideal images. Run this movie in your mind over and over - forwards, backwards, in slow-motion, as a member of the audience, through your eyes.

Be ready to contribute this image to the audience in the group discussion that follows.

Review the activity instructions:

'If you are going to give a presentation in a sales meeting, in a speech, or in an interview, picture a range of possible scenarios. Begin with an ideal outcome.

Imagine you're performing in top shape with things happening exactly as you want them to.

Then picture a mediocre outcome, with things happening close to the ideal but not quite.

Then visualise the worst possible outcome with you stumbling over yourself. In the process of rehearsing these scenarios, you prepare yourself for mishaps and problems.

Then once you have worked through the possibilities, focus on the ideal images. Allow yourself to perform marvellously.

Run this movie in your mind over and over, forwards, backwards, in slow motion, as a member of the audience, through your eyes.'

Ask delegates to make detailed notes on these images.

After 10-15 minutes go around the room and ask each delegate to share their images and goals.

Discussion Points

- Did the images and scenes begin to 'flow' after you had focused on a goal?

- How much detail were you able to generate?

CLUSTERING

Format:	*Individually/Group review*
Type:	*Session starter/Climate changer*
Time:	*20-30 minutes*
Resources:	*OHP, flip-chart, training resource ref: 85*
Suitable for:	*All levels*

Purpose

To allow delegates to practise a method of thinking and organising our thoughts.

Procedure

Ask delegates to work individually and be ready to contribute their results to the group discussion that will follow.

Introduce the exercise with the following short summary:

'If reading exercises your mind by making you analyse and synthesise ideas, writing exercises your mind by making you clearly formulate and express ideas. An innovative approach to help you think with words, developed by author Gabriel Lusser Rico, is to organise words in a visual tree diagram. Rico called the technique clustering.'

Clustering allows your mind to wander freely around concepts. Because the structure is open ended you can add ideas anywhere. Like a plant growing outwards, the tree structure encourages ideas to take root, develop and branch out.

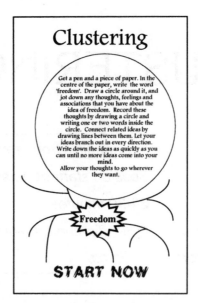

Clustering

Get a pen and a piece of paper. In the centre of the paper, write the word 'freedom'. Draw a circle around it, and jot down any thoughts, feelings and associations that you have about the idea of freedom. Record these thoughts by drawing a circle and writing one or two words inside the circle. Connect related ideas by drawing lines between them. Let your ideas branch out in every direction. Write down the ideas as quickly as you can until no more ideas come into your mind.
Allow your thoughts to go wherever they want.

Freedom

START NOW

While the presence of one central thought keeps your ideas focused, the branching structure allows your ideas to reach out freely. You splash ideas onto a page, writing as quickly as thoughts appear, keeping closely related ideas clustered together and distantly related ideas separate. The various ideas are clearly separate, yet connected. Because the lines show relationships you can in a glance see the relative importance of each."

Perhaps demonstrate this by running a short cluster on the flip-chart.

Ask delegates to work on their chart. After 10-15 minutes go around the room and ask each delegate to share their cluster drawings. Repeat with different topics. (Exercise can also be run with delegates working in pairs.)

Discussion Points

- What are the advantages over normal note-taking methods?

- Are the thoughts that arise surprising?

- Is it easier or faster to think in this way?

- What advantages does it offer when reviewing your notes?

- Suggest that it might be useful to make notes and organise our thinking using this method more often.

Caption

Competition

Format:	*Pairs*
Type:	*Climate changer/Energiser*
Time:	*10-15 minutes or as required*
Resources:	*OHP Slide, flip-chart, training resources ref: 86, 87, 88*
Suitable for:	*All levels*

Purpose

To practise humour and creativity.

Procedure

The OHP slides/handouts are a series of pictures missing a caption or heading. They make an excellent addition to any training course, presentation or group event, adding both humour and imagination. It is usually possible to create captions that are appropriate to your course or topic.

Ask delegates to work in pairs on this exercise, which will test their imagination and humour.

Either display as OHP slides or distribute as handouts.

Allow 10-15 minutes and then go around the group asking delegates to read out their caption or headlines.

Section 7: Word Power

Doublets

Anagrams

Appended Anagrams

Alphabet Advance

Circle of Thought

Spontaneous Speechmaking

Can You Say It Another Way?

A to Z

Word Creation

Clear Descriptions

Limerick Competition

Word Power

A Funny Thing Happened on the Way to the Training Course...

Story Creation

DOUBLETS

Format:	Pairs
Type:	Climate changer/Icebreaker
Time:	10 minutes or as required
Resources:	OHP, flip-chart, training resources ref: 89, 90
Suitable for:	All levels

Purpose

To allow delegates to work in pairs and practise verbal dexterity and thinking.

Procedure

Review the following notes with the group:

The doublets puzzle was invented by Lewis Carroll. This is how he described it:

'The rules of the puzzle are simple enough. Two words are proposed of the same length, and the puzzle consists in linking these together by interposing other words, each of which shall differ from the next word in one letter only.

That is to say, one letter may be changed in one of the given words, then one letter in the word so obtained, and so on, until we arrive at another given word. The letters must not be inter-changed among themselves, but each must keep its own place.

As an example the word "head" may be changed into "tail" by interposing the words "heal, teal, tell, tall" . I call the two given words "a doublet", the interposed words "links" and the entire series "a chain". It is perhaps, needless to state that it is *de rigueur* that the links should be English words, such as might be used in good society.

Perhaps write the example above on the flip-chart.

Next, ask delegates to work in pairs, trying to link the words as quickly as possible.

Write the first word on the flip-chart, or display the slide revealing one line (word exercise) at a time, or distribute as a handout. Move quickly, progressing as soon as most or all delegates have completed each exercise.

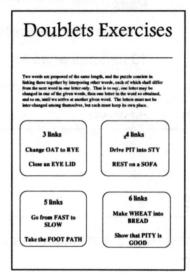

Doublets Exercises

Two words are proposed of the same length, and the puzzle consists in linking these together by interposing other words, each of which shall differ from the next word in one letter only. That is to say, one letter may be changed in one of the given words, then one letter in the word so obtained, and so on, until we arrive at another given word. The letters must not be inter-changed among themselves, but each must keep its own place.

3 links

Change OAT to RYE

Close an EYE LID

4 links

Drive PIT into STY

REST on a SOFA

5 links

Go from FAST to SLOW

Take the FOOT PATH

6 links

Make WHEAT into BREAD

Show that PITY is GOOD

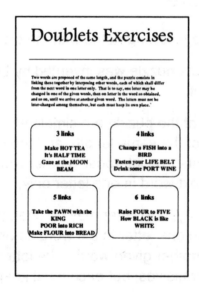

Doublets Exercises

Two words are proposed of the same length, and the puzzle consists in linking these together by interposing other words, each of which shall differ from the next word in one letter only. That is to say, one letter may be changed in one of the given words, then on letter in the word so obtained, and so on, until we arrive at another given word. The letters must not be inter-changed among themselves, but each must keep its own place.'

3 links

Make HOT TEA
It's HALF TIME
Gaze at the MOON BEAM

4 links

Change a FISH into a BIRD
Fasten your LIFE BELT
Drink some PORT WINE

5 links

Take the PAWN with the KING
POOR into RICH
Make FLOUR into BREAD

6 links

Raise FOUR to FIVE
How BLACK is like WHITE

Answers:

3 links

Change OAT to RYE-*OAT, rat, rot, roe, RYE*

Close an EYE LID-*EYE, dye, die, did, LID*

Make HOT TEA-*HOT, sot, set, sea, TEA*

It's HALF TIME-*HALF, hale, tale, tile, TIME*

Gaze at the MOON BEAM-*MOON, moan, mean, bean, BEAM*

4 links

Drive PIG into a STY-*PIG, wig, wag, way, say, STY*

REST on a SOFA-*REST, lest, lost, loft, soft, SOFA*

Change a FISH into a BIRD-*FISH, fist, gist, girt, gird, BIRD*

Fasten your LIFE BELT-*LIFE, lift, list, lest, best, BELT*

Drink some PORT WINE-*PORT, part, pant, pint, pine, WINE*

5 links

Go from FAST to SLOW-*FAST, last, lost, loot, soot, slot, SLOW*

Take the FOOT PATH-*FOOT, fort, fore, fare, fate, pate, PATH*

Take the PAWN with the KING-*PAWN, paws, pans, pins, pink, kink, KING*

Transform POOR into RICH-*POOR, boor, book, rook, rock, rick, RICH*

Bake some FLOUR into BREAD-*FLOUR, floor, flood, blood, brood, broad, BREAD*

6 links

Make WHEAT into BREAD-*WHEAT, cheat, cheap, cheep, creep, creed, breed, BREAD*

Show that PITY is GOOD-*PITY, pits, pins, fins, find, fond, food, GOOD*

Raise FOUR to FIVE-*FOUR, foul, fool, foot, fort, fore, fire, FIVE*

How BLACK is like WHITE-*BLACK, blank, blink, clink, chink, chine, whine, WHITE*

ANAGRAMS

Format:	*Pairs*
Type:	*Climate changer/Icebreaker*
Time:	*10 minutes or as required*
Resources:	*OHP, flip-chart, training resources ref: 91, 92*
Suitable for:	*All levels*

Purpose

To sharpen thinking and get delegates working in pairs or small groups.

Procedure

Anagrams require complex sorting of letter patterns. The brain creates a random word, and then checks with memory to see if it is valid. For example:

Reshuffle the letters of the word ASPIRANT and you can find the word PARTISAN.

Ask delegates to work in pairs and set delegates the task of finding one anagram from each word in the shortest time possible.

Distribute handout or display as an OHP slide.

Anagrams/1

Reshuffle the letters of the word ASPIRANT and you can find the word PARTISAN. How long will it take you to find new words from the following list?

TREASON

WANDER

BESTIARY

MEDUSA

MASCULINE

DICTIONARY

Anagrams/2

Reshuffle the letters of the word ASPIRANT and you can find the word PARTISAN. How long will it take you to find new words from the following list?

DIRECTOR

CATECHISM

LEOPARD

CONSIDERATE

EXCITATION

LEGISLATOR

Alternative: Set a time limit of, say, 10 minutes, and ask delegates to find as many anagrams as possible, making sure they have at least one new word from each word.

Discussion Points

- Do some people do this exercise more quickly than others?

- What was the mental 'sorting' strategy that you used?

- Do you have an approach from which others might learn?

- How can these analytical skills be useful in other areas?

Answers:

TREASON - Senator

WANDER - Warden

BESTIARY - Sybarite

MEDUSA - Amused

MASCULINE - Calumnies

DICTIONARY - Indicatory

DIRECTOR - Creditor

CATECHISM - Schematic

LEOPARD - Paroled

CONSIDERATE - Desecration

EXCITATION - Intoxicate

LEGISLATOR - Allegorist

APPENDED ANAGRAMS

Format:	Pairs
Type:	Climate changer/Icebreaker
Time:	15-20 minutes or as required
Resources:	OHP, flip-chart, training resources ref: 93, 94
Suitable for:	All levels

Purpose

To sharpen thinking and get delegates working in pairs or small groups.

Procedure

Anagrams require complex sorting of letter patterns. The brain creates a random word, and then checks with memory to see if it is valid. For example:

Add the letter C to a word, then rearrange the letters to find a new word. Add another C, resort the letters, and find yet another word. For example, add C to OIL and create COIL. Add a C to COIL and create COLIC.

Ask delegates to work in pairs and set them the task of finding one anagram from each word in the shortest time possible.

Distribute handout or display as an OHP slide.

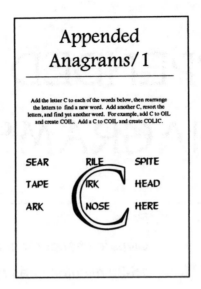

Appended Anagrams/1

Add the letter C to each of the words below, then rearrange
the letters to find a new word. Add another C, resort the
letters, and find yet another word. For example, add C to OIL
and create COIL. Add a C to COIL and create COLIC.

SEAR	RILE	SPITE
TAPE	IRK	HEAD
ARK	NOSE	HERE

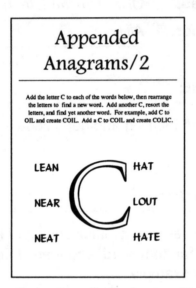

Appended Anagrams/2

Add the letter C to each of the words below, then rearrange
the letters to find a new word. Add another C, resort the
letters, and find yet another word. For example, add C to
OIL and create COIL. Add a C to COIL and create COLIC.

LEAN	HAT
NEAR	LOUT
NEAT	HATE

Alternative: Set a time limit of, say, 10 minutes, and ask delegates
to find as many anagrams as possible, making sure they have at
lease one new word from each word.

Discussion Points

➧ Do some people do this exercise more quickly than others?

➧ Do you have an approach from which others might learn?

➧ How can these analytical skills be useful in other areas?

Answers:

HAT - Chat, Catch.

LOUT - Clout, Occult.

HATE - Cheat, Cachet.

SEAR - Scare, Scarce.

TAPE - Epact, Accept.

ARK - Rack, Crack.

SPITE - Septic, Sceptic.

HEAD - Ached, Cached.

HERE - Cheer, Creche.

RILE - Relic, Circle.

IRK - Rick, Crick.

NOSE - Scone, Sconce.

LEAN - Lance, Cancel.

NEAR - Crane, Cancer.

NEAT - Enact, Accent.

ALPHABET
ADVANCE

Format:	*Pairs*
Type:	*Climate changer/Icebreaker*
Time:	*10 minutes or as required*
Resources:	*OHP, flip-chart, training resource ref: 95*
Suitable for:	*All levels*

Purpose

To sharpen thinking and get delegates working in pairs or small groups.

Procedure

This exercise is a variation on the theme of anagrams and involves shifting backwards or forwards through the alphabet.

For example, if you shift each of the letters of the word COLD three positions forward, so that the letter C becomes F, O becomes R, L becomes O, and D becomes G, you arrive at a new word, FROG. In the list of words given, some must be advanced, and others reversed. Can you figure out the other words?

Ask delegates to work in pairs and set them the task of finding one other word from each word in the shortest time possible by advancing or reversing letters.

Distribute the handout or display as an OHP slide.

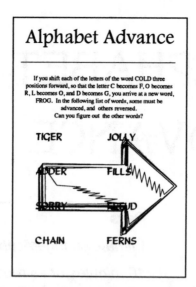

Alphabet Advance

If you shift each of the letters of the word COLD three positions forward, so that the letter C becomes F, O becomes R, L becomes O, and D becomes G, you arrive at a new word, FROG. In the following list of words, some must be advanced, and others reversed.

Can you figure out the other words?

TIGER   JOLLY

ADDER   FILLS

SORRY   FREUD

CHAIN   FERNS

Alternative: Set a time limit of, say, 10 minutes, and ask delegates to find as many anagrams as possible, making sure they have at least one new word from each word.

(NB: All letters are moved the same number of steps each.)

Discussion Points

➲ Do some people do this exercise more quickly than others?

➲ What was the mental 'sorting' strategy that you used?

➲ Do you have an approach from which others might learn?

➲ How can these analytical skills be useful in other areas?

Answers:

TIGER - Pecan (four letters back).

JOLLY - Cheer (seven letters back).

ADDER - Beefs (one letter forward).

FILLS - Lorry (six letters forward).

SORRY - Mills (six letters back).

FREUD - Cobra (three letters back).

CHAIN - Ingot (six letters forward).

FERNS - Banjo (four letters back).

CIRCLE OF THOUGHT

Format:	*Pairs*
Type:	*Climate changer/Icebreaker*
Time:	*10 minutes or as required*
Resources:	*OHP, flip-chart, training resource ref: 96*
Suitable for:	*All levels*

Purpose

To practise quick thinking and get delegates working in pairs or small groups.

Procedure

This exercise is a variation on the theme of shifting backwards or forward through the alphabet (previous exercise).

Distribute handout or display as an OHP slide.

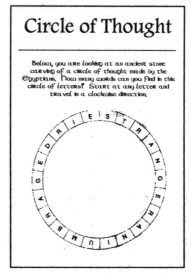

Set a time limit, say 10 minutes, and ask delegates to work as quickly as they can and see how many words they can find in this circle of letters.

Start at any letter and travel in a clockwise direction.

Example: *Starting at the top, and travelling clockwise, you can find the word 'STRANGER', and so on.*

When the time is up, review delegates' totals and nominate a winner.

Discussion Points

● Do some people do this exercise more quickly than others?

● What was the mental 'sorting' strategy that you used?

● Do you have an approach from which others might learn?

● How can these analytical skills be useful in other areas?

Answers:

There are at least twenty words in the circle.

Umbra	*Driest,*
Anger	*Range,*
Geranium	*Rage,*
Ran	*Raged*
Rag	*Umbrage*
Brag	*Ranger*
Age	*Stranger*
Aged	*Estrange*
Era	*An*
Dries	*Rang*

SPONTANEOUS SPEECHMAKING

Format:	*Group*
Type:	*Climate changer/Energiser*
Time:	*10-15 minutes or as required*
Resources:	*OHP, flip-chart, training resource ref: 97*
Suitable for:	*All levels*

Purpose

To practise quick thinking and raise energy levels in a group.

Procedure

Explain that this exercise is about quick thinking.

Set delegates the task of making four statements aloud and spontaneously about or around or using the words listed on the handout.

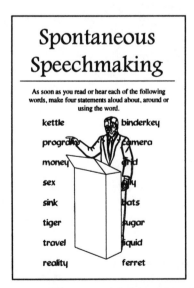

Move around the group quickly, setting each delegate a different word in turn.

If any delegate cannot make four statements, the same word moves on to the next delegate until four statements are achieved.

The previous word must also be used in the new story.

Emphasise that the statements can be about anything, so long as they contain the word four times and the previous word at least once.

Alternative: Repeat the exercise, this time giving delegates two or three words each to include in one statement.

Discussion Points

- What stops us from being spontaneous?

- Were the results (the statements) more or less creative and interesting than a planned speech?

- How can we build more spontaneity into our work, and what are the advantages of this?

CAN YOU SAY IT ANOTHER WAY?

Format:	*Pairs*
Type:	*Climate changer/Energiser*
Time:	*10-15 minutes or as required*
Resources:	*OHP, flip-chart, training resource ref: 98, 99*
Suitable for:	*All levels*

Purpose

To practise quick thinking and raise energy levels in a group.

Procedure

Ask delegates to work in pairs on this exercise, which will test their depth of word usage or vocabulary.

Our ability to express our ideas and interpret our words is often constrained by the words or language we use. For example, in this country we have two or three words to describe 'snow', Eskimos have over 60.

Human beings who have the gift of speaking have at their disposal a rich and varied vocabulary as well as the knowledge of where and when to use words. They can find the word that expresses the exact shade of meaning they wish to convey.

Distribute the handout or display as an OHP.

Can You Say It Another Way?/1

Human beings who have the gift of speaking have at their disposal a rich and varied vocabulary as well as the knowledge of where and when to use words. They can find the word that expresses the exact shade of meaning they wish to convey. How many words or phrases can you come up with that mean the same or almost the same as the following words? (Aim for at least ten of each.)

Foolish

Important

Sad

Friend

Fearful

Can you say it Another Way?/2

How many words or phrases can you come up with that mean the same or almost the same as the following words? (Aim for at least ten of each.)

Attractive

Self assured

Happy

Wonderful

Relaxed

Set the task : *'How many words or phrases can you come up with that mean the same or almost the same as the following words? (Aim for at least ten of each.)'*

Word	Example
Foolish	- idiotic, slow-witted, short-sighted
Important	- weighty, eventful, major, significant
Sad	- sombre, down, blue, melancholic
Friend	- comrade, chum, mate, companion
Fearful	- timid, anxious, lily-livered, yellow
Humorous	- funny, a riot, witty
Attractive	- alluring, fascinating, appealing
Self-assured	- cool, confident, brassy, certain

After ten minutes or so, review each word in turn, listing alternatives and variations on the flip-chart.

Discussion Points

⊃ Did it surprise you how many different words you could generate?

⊃ How much variety do we actually use in our conversation, compared to the richness we could use?

A TO Z

Format:	Pairs
Type:	Climate changer/Energiser
Time:	10-15 minutes or as required
Resources:	Flip-chart
Suitable for:	All levels

Purpose

To practise quick thinking and raise energy levels in a group.

Procedure

Ask delegates to work in pairs on this exercise, which will test their depth of word usage or vocabulary, and their imagination.

Like the last exercise, our ability to express our ideas and interpret our words in an imaginative way can help us communicate better.

Human beings who have the gift of speaking have at their disposal a rich and varied vocabulary as well as the knowledge of where and when to use words. They can find the word that expresses the exact shade of meaning they wish to convey.

Set the task, selecting one or more of the words or categories listed (these can be written on the flip-chart if preferred):

'Test your ability to come up with words by compiling a list of twenty six related words in alphabetical order.'

For example:

Occupations	architect, baker, chemist…
Cities	Albuquerque, Brussels, Cairo…
Musical instruments	accordion, banjo, cello…
Animals	aardvark, buzzard, crane…
Foods	artichoke, bread, cranberry…

Compile similar lists from your own special field of interest, such as names of plants, insects, pop songs or streets, countries, cities, towns, products, authors, books, television programmes, forms of transport etc.

Discussion Points

- Did it surprise you how many different words you could generate?

- How much variety do we actually use in our conversation, compared to the richness we could use?

WORD CREATION

Format:	*Pairs*
Type:	*Climate changer/Energiser*
Time:	*10-15 minutes or as required*
Resources:	*OHP, flip-chart, training resources ref: 100, 101*
Suitable for:	*All levels*

Purpose

To practise imagination and thinking based on word imagining.

Procedure

Ask delegates to work in pairs on this exercise, which will test their imagination and word usage.

Introduce the exercise by highlighting how some sounds are either onomatopoeic or sound or look appropriate to their meaning. For example, 'sizzle', 'quick', 'pop'. Like in the last exercise, our ability to express our ideas and interpret our words in an imaginative way can help us communicate better.

Set the task by distributing the handout or displaying as an OHP, selecting one or more of the words or categories listed (these can be written on the flip-chart if preferred). You may distribute different works to certain pairs or groups.

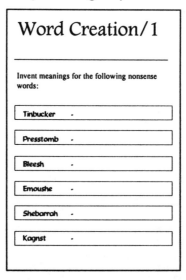

Word Creation/1

Invent meanings for the following nonsense words:

Tinbucker -

Presstomb -

Bleesh -

Emoushe -

Sheborrah -

Kagnst -

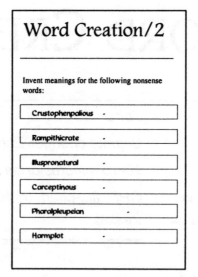

Word Creation/2

Invent meanings for the following nonsense words:

Crustophenpalious	-
Rampithicrate	-
Illuspronatural	-
Corceptinous	-
Pharalpleupeian	-
Harmplot	-

After a short time, regain delegates' attention and go around gaining possible definitions.

(All the words are fictitious, we think!)

CLEAR DESCRIPTIONS

Format:	*Pairs*
Type:	*Climate changer/Energiser*
Time:	*10-15 minutes or as required*
Resources:	*OHP, flip-chart, training resources ref: 102, 103*
Suitable for:	*All levels*

Purpose

To practise imaginative thinking and word precision.

Procedure

Ask delegates to work in pairs on this exercise, which will test their communication skills and word usage.

Set the task, by distributing the handout or displaying it as an OHP, selecting one or more of the words or categories (these can be written on the flip-chart if preferred):

Discussion Points

⊃ Was this exercise harder than expected?

⊃ What made it difficult?

⊃ Who created the best description?

⊃ What can this teach about how we communicate ideas, concepts and plans to others?

LIMERICK COMPETITION

Format:	*Pairs*
Type:	*Climate changer/Energiser*
Time:	*20-25 minutes or as required*
Resources:	*OHP, flip-chart, training resource ref: 104*
Suitable for:	*All levels*

Purpose

To get delegates working in pairs and to practise verbal creativity.

Procedure

Ask delegates to work in pairs on this exercise, which will test their imagination and lyrical ability.

Introduce the exercise by stating that a limerick is one of the oldest forms of rhyme and poetry and is found the world over.

Next, set the task, by distributing the handout or displaying as an OHP, and ask delegates to select one or more of the first lines. (These can be written on the flip-chart if preferred), and to make up a limerick .

Limerick Competition

Make up a limerick using one of the following first lines: (If you have time, produce as many as you can.)

There was once a Vicar named Gus...

A travelling salesman rang twice...

A girl who weighed too much...

There was a smart lad from Madras...

There was a young man from Paris..

Allow 10-15 minutes and then go around the group asking delegates to read out their limerick or transfer them to the flip-chart. Ask the group to vote for their favourite.

Discussion Points

○ Was it hard or easy to write limericks?

○ How can you apply this to your communication skills?

○ Does the fact that the verse might be nonsense detract from its charm?

WORD POWER

Format:	*Pairs*
Type:	*Climate changer/Energiser*
Time:	*15-20 minutes or as required*
Resources:	*OHP, flip-chart, training resource ref: 105*
Suitable for:	*All levels*

Purpose

To get delegates working in pairs and to practise creativity in word usage.

Procedure

Ask delegates to work in pairs on this exercise, which will test their imagination.

Introduce the exercise by giving examples of how words can contain a certain 'feel' or radiance of their own, particularly when used in marketing (e.g.: Daz, Bentley, Jaguar, Obsession, Power, Guns and Roses etc.)

Next, set the task, by distributing the handout or displaying as an OHP, selecting one or more of the categories listed (these can be written on the flip-chart if preferred):

Word Power

There seems to be the right name for just about everything. Test your ability to create innovative names that grab people's attention. Make up names for the following (if time allows, create several names for each).

- ✓ a perfume
- ✓ a fashion line
- ✓ an introduction service
- ✓ a wheelbarrow
- ✓ a pop song
- ✓ a pop group
- ✓ a pet dog
- ✓ a computer company
- ✓ a new model of sports car
- ✓ a stage name for a singer

Allow 10-15 minutes and then go around the group asking delegates to read out their answers or transfer them to the flip-chart. Ask the group to vote for their favourites.

Discussion Points

- How can the correct choice of words improve our communication?

- Is it possible to create interest and a certain perception by the words that we use to either name something or describe it?

A FUNNY THING HAPPENED ON THE WAY TO THE TRAINING COURSE...

Format:	*Pairs/Syndicates*
Type:	*Climate changer/Energiser*
Time:	*20 minutes or as required*
Resources:	*OHP, flip-chart, training resource ref: 106*
Suitable for:	*All levels*

Purpose

To get delegates working in pairs and to practise creativity.

Procedure

Ask delegates to work in pairs on this exercise, which will test their imagination and joke-writing ability.

Introduce the exercise by asking delegates 'What makes a joke funny?' Run a short discussion around this theme, perhaps asking for examples of different types of humorous stories or jokes. A joke usually has an incongruent, unexpected or unusual twist or ending, or is delivered in a certain manner at which humour can arise, again mismatching verbal and non-verbal communication.

Next, set the task, by distributing the handout or displaying as an OHP, or selecting one or more of the categories listed (these can be written on the flip-chart if preferred):

A Funny Thing Happened...

Make up a joke or humorous story from the following subject:

- ⮑ a funny thing happened on the way to the training course...
- ⮑ a traffic warden and a gorilla
- ⮑ an actress and a vicar
- ⮑ a dog walks into a pub
- ⮑ a salesman in heaven/hell
- ⮑ a political figure
- ⮑ a chef and a police officer
- ⮑ a fisherman in front of the gates of heaven.

Allow 10-15 minutes and then go around the group asking delegates to read out their answers or to transfer them to a flip-chart. Ask the group to vote for their favourites.

Discussion Points

- ● Did the same or similar jokes appear?

- ● Were the same 'devices' used, changing characters and settings?

- ● What is the role of humour in building rapport in a group of people?

- ● Was it harder or easier than you expected to write jokes deliberately?

STORY CREATION

Format:	*Pairs*
Type:	*Climate changer/Energiser*
Time:	*30 minutes or as required*
Resources:	*OHP , flip-chart, training resource ref: 107*
Suitable for:	*All levels*

Purpose

To get delegates working together and to practise creativity.

Procedure

Ask delegates to work in pairs on this exercise, which will test their imagination and creativity.

Introduce the exercise by asking delegates if they have ever made-up or written stories (since leaving school).

The skill of being able to connect key themes, characters and situations is useful, not only in fiction but also in conversation, communication and presenting.

Next, set the task, by distributing the handout or displaying as an OHP. Delegates can choose whether to make the stories simple or bizarre, funny or serious. Delegates can choose four words, one from each column, as the main basis for their story.

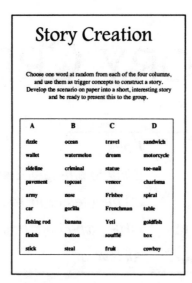

Story Creation

Choose one word at random from each of the four columns, and use them as trigger concepts to construct a story. Develop the scenario on paper into a short, interesting story and be ready to present this to the group.

A	B	C	D
fizzle	ocean	travel	sandwich
wallet	watermelon	dream	motorcycle
sideline	criminal	statue	toe-nail
pavement	topcoat	veneer	charisma
army	nose	Frisbee	spiral
car	gorilla	Frenchman	table
fishing rod	banana	Yeti	goldfish
finish	button	soufflé	box
stick	steal	fruit	cowboy

Allow 10-15 minutes and then go around the group asking delegates to read out their stories. Ask the group to vote for their favourites.

Discussion Points

- Did the same or similar stories appear?

- Were the same 'devices' used, changing characters and settings?

- What is the role of 'story telling' in building rapport and in a group of people?

- Was it harder or easier than you expected to write stories?

Section 8: Lateral Thinking Puzzles

The Turkish Bath Mystery

Antony and Cleopatra

A Remarkable Journey

The Abyssinian Postal Service

The Hotel Detective

Concorde

World War I

King George IV

The Dream

The Man in the Hotel

Short Roads

The Plane Hijacker

Section 8: Lateral Thinking Puzzles

THE TURKISH BATH MYSTERY

Format:	*Pairs/Individual*
Type:	*Climate changer/Energiser*
Time:	*10-15 minutes or as required*
Resources:	*OHP, flip-chart, training resource ref: 108*
Suitable for:	*All levels*

Purpose

To practise creative and lateral thinking.

Procedure

Ask delegates to work in pairs on this exercise, which will test their lateral thinking ability and creativity.

Either read out the story, display as an OHP or distribute as a handout.

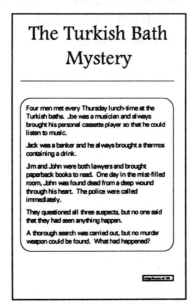

The Turkish Bath Mystery

Four men met every Thursday lunch-time at the Turkish baths. Joe was a musician and always brought his personal cassette player so that he could listen to music.

Jack was a banker and he always brought a thermos containing a drink.

Jim and John were both lawyers and brought paperback books to read. One day in the mist-filled room, John was found dead from a deep wound through his heart. The police were called immediately.

They questioned all three suspects, but no one said that they had seen anything happen.

A thorough search was carried out, but no murder weapon could be found. What had happened?

Allow 10-15 minutes and then go around the group asking delegates to read out their answers or conclusion.

You might choose to provide short yes or no answers to delegates' questions, although be careful not to lead them too quickly to the answer. Encourage delegates to explore all possible options, thinking as laterally and creatively as possible.

As an alternative format, delegates can work on the problem in syndicates, creating more of a group interaction and team-building exercise.

The Clues

Q: Was John murdered by one of his three companions?

A: Yes.

Q: Was he stabbed by one of them?

A: Yes.

Q: Did the murderer bring the weapon into the baths with him?

A: Yes.

Q: Could the police have found the weapon if they had searched harder?

A: No.

Answer:

John was murdered by Jack, who brought an ice dagger into the Turkish baths in his thermos flask. The dagger melted away after the murder, leaving no clue.

ANTONY AND CLEOPATRA

Format:	*Pairs/Individual*
Type:	*Climate changer/Energiser*
Time:	*10-15 minutes or as required*
Resources:	*OHP, flip-chart, training resource ref: 109*
Suitable for:	*All levels*

Purpose

To practise creative and lateral thinking.

Procedure

Ask delegates to work in pairs on this exercise, which will test their lateral thinking ability and creativity.

Either read out the story, display as an OHP or distribute as a handout.

Antony And Cleopatra

Antony and Cleopatra are lying dead on the floor in an Egyptian villa. Nearby is a broken bowl. There are no marks on the bodies and they were not poisoned. No person was in the villa when they died. How did they die?

Allow 10-15 minutes and then go around the group asking delegates to read out their answers or conclusion.

You might choose to provide short yes or no answers to delegates' questions, although be careful not to lead them too quickly to the answer. Encourage delegates to explore all possible options, thinking as laterally and creatively as possible.

As an alternative format, delegates can work on the problem in syndicates, creating more of a group interaction and team-building exercise.

The Clues

This is an old one, although it can prove a little difficult if you have not heard it before.

The most fruitful lines of questioning are those that try to establish the exact cause and circumstances of death. To cut a long story short, it can be said that their deaths followed the accidental breaking of the bowl. The bowl had contained water.

The Answer:

Antony and Cleopatra were goldfish. They died when their bowl was knocked over by a rather clumsy guard dog.

A REMARKABLE JOURNEY

Format:	*Pairs/Individual*
Type:	*Climate changer/Energiser*
Time:	*10-15 minutes or as required*
Resources:	*OHP , flip-chart, training resource ref: 110*
Suitable for:	*All levels*

Purpose

To practise creative and lateral thinking.

Procedure

Ask delegates to work in pairs on this exercise, which will test their lateral thinking ability and creativity.

Either read out the story, display as an OHP or distribute as a handout.

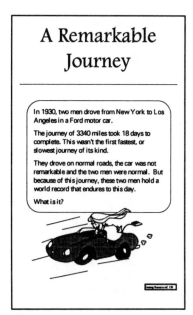

> ### A Remarkable Journey
>
> In 1930, two men drove from New York to Los Angeles in a Ford motor car.
>
> The journey of 3340 miles took 18 days to complete. This wasn't the first fastest, or slowest journey of its kind.
>
> They drove on normal roads, the car was not remarkable and the two men were normal. But because of this journey, these two men hold a world record that endures to this day.
>
> What is it?

Allow 10-15 minutes and then go around the group asking delegates to read out their answers or conclusion.

You might choose to provide short yes or no answers to delegates' questions, although be careful not to lead them too quickly to the answer. Encourage delegates to explore all possible options, thinking as lateral and creatively as possible.

As an alternative format, delegates can work on the problem in syndicates, creating more of a group interaction and team-building exercise.

The Clues

An important point in the description is that they hold a world record. It is not just a record for going from New York to Los Angeles. The distance and manner of the journey are what count.

It is a remarkable record. It does not involve silly aspects of the car or the men. If in doubt think laterally!

The Answer:

They hold the world record for the longest journey driven in reverse. Charles Creighton and James Hargis drove their Ford Model A in reverse all the way from New York to Los Angeles between 26 July and 16 August 1930. They then drove back to New York, again in reverse.

THE ABYSSINIAN POSTAL SERVICE

Format:	*Pairs/Individual*
Type:	*Climate changer/Energiser*
Time:	*10-15 minutes or as required*
Resources:	*OHP, flip-chart, training resource ref: 111*
Suitable for:	*All levels*

Purpose

To practise creative and lateral thinking.

Procedure

Ask delegates to work in pairs on this exercise, which will test their lateral thinking ability and creativity.

Either read out the story, display as an OHP or distribute as a handout.

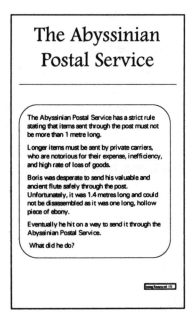

The Abyssinian Postal Service

The Abyssinian Postal Service has a strict rule stating that items sent through the post must not be more than 1 metre long.

Longer items must be sent by private carriers, who are notorious for their expense, inefficiency, and high rate of loss of goods.

Boris was desperate to send his valuable and ancient flute safely through the post. Unfortunately, it was 1.4 metres long and could not be disassembled as it was one long, hollow piece of ebony.

Eventually he hit on a way to send it through the Abyssinian Postal Service.

What did he do?

Training Resource 111

Allow 10-15 minutes and then go around the group asking delegates to read out their answers or conclusion.

You might choose to provide short yes or no answers to delegates' questions, although be careful not to lead them too quickly to the answer. Encourage delegates to explore all possible options, thinking as laterally and creatively as possible.

As an alternative format, delegates can work on the problem in syndicates, creating more of a group interaction and team-building exercise.

The Clues

Q: Did he break or bend the flute in any way?

A: No.

Q: Did Boris send it through the Abyssinian Postal Service?

A: Yes.

Q: Did he send it in a container that met the rules of not being longer than one metre?

A: Yes.

Q: Do the Abyssinian Postal Service officials measure items correctly with a tape measure along both sides?

A: Yes.

The Answer:

Boris placed the flute diagonally in a suitcase that measured 1 metre by 1 metre. This suitcase was quite acceptable to the officials because its sides measured 1 metre. From corner to corner it measured 1.414 metres-the square root of two. Equally, if his flute had measured 1.7 metres, he could have fitted it across the diagonal of a box whose sides were 1 metre long. The diagonal of a cube is the square root of three times its side, 1.73 metres

THE HOTEL DETECTIVE

Format:	*Pairs/Individual*
Type:	*Climate changer/Energiser*
Time:	*10-15 minutes or as required*
Resources:	*OHP, flip-chart, training resource ref: 112*
Suitable for:	*All levels*

Purpose

To practise creative and lateral thinking.

Procedure

Ask delegates to work in pairs on this exercise, which will test their lateral thinking ability and creativity. Either read out the story, display it as an OHP or distribute it as a handout.

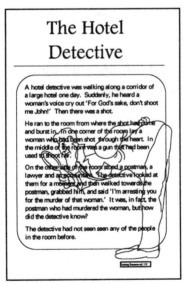

The Hotel Detective

A hotel detective was walking along a corridor of a large hotel one day. Suddenly, he heard a woman's voice cry out 'For God's sake, don't shoot me John!' Then there was a shot.

He ran to the room from where the shot had come and burst in. In one corner of the room lay a woman who had been shot through the heart. In the middle of the room was a gun that had been used to shoot her.

On the other side of the room stood a postman, a lawyer and an accountant. The detective looked at them for a moment and then walked towards the postman, grabbed him, and said 'I'm arresting you for the murder of that woman.' It was, in fact, the postman who had murdered the woman, but how did the detective know?

The detective had not seen seen any of the people in the room before.

Allow 10-15 minutes and then go around the group asking delegates to read out their answers or conclusion.

You might choose to provide short yes or no answers to delegates questions, although be careful not to lead them too quickly to the

answer. Encourage delegates to explore all possible options, thinking as laterally and creatively as possible.

As an alternative format, delegates can work on the problem in syndicates, creating more of a group interaction and team-building exercise.

The Clues

Q: Was the profession of each of the three suspects immediately apparent?

A: No.

Q: Was each wearing normal working clothes?

A: Yes.

Q: Were they wearing name tags or other means of identification?

A: No.

Q: Was it something to do with the position or use of the gun?

A: No.

Q: Would it have been obvious to most people who the murderer was?

A: Yes.

The Answer:

The lawyer and the accountant were women. The postman was therefore the only person who could have been called John.

CONCORDE

Format:	*Pairs/Individual*
Type:	*Climate changer/Energiser*
Time:	*10-15 minutes or as required*
Resources:	*OHP, flip-chart, training resource ref: 113*
Suitable for:	*All levels*

Purpose

To practise creative and lateral thinking.

Procedure

Ask delegates to work in pairs on this exercise, which will test their lateral thinking ability and creativity.

Either read out the story, display as an OHP or distribute as a handout.

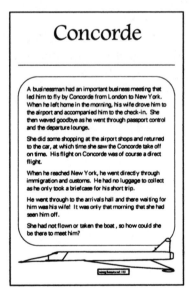

Allow 10-15 minutes and then go around the group asking delegates to read out their answers or conclusion.

You might choose to provide short yes or no answers to delegates questions, although be careful not to lead them too quickly too the

answer. Encourage delegates to explore all possible options, thinking as laterally and creatively as possible.

As an alternative format, delegates can work on the problem in syndicates, creating more of a group interaction and team-building exercise.

The Clues

This is another problem that repays the questioning of all assumptions made.

Q: Did his wife travel (other than from home to the airport)?

A: No.

Q: Was she in New York to meet him?

A: Yes.

Q: Was she in London to see him off?

A: No.

Q: Did someone else see him off from London?

A: No.

The Answer:

He lived in New York. His wife saw him off from New York in the morning and greeted him on his return in the evening.

WORLD WAR I

Format:	*Pairs/Individual*
Type:	*Climate changer/Energiser*
Time:	*10-15 minutes or as required*
Resources:	*OHP, flip-chart, training resource ref: 114*
Suitable for:	*All levels*

Purpose

To practise creative and lateral thinking.

Procedure

Ask delegates to work in pairs on this exercise, which will test their lateral thinking ability and creativity.

Either read out the story, display it as an OHP or distribute it as a handout.

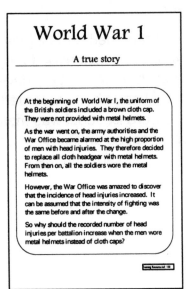

World War 1

A true story

At the beginning of World War I, the uniform of the British soldiers included a brown cloth cap. They were not provided with metal helmets.

As the war went on, the army authorities and the War Office became alarmed at the high proportion of men with head injuries. They therefore decided to replace all cloth headgear with metal helmets. From then on, all the soldiers wore the metal helmets.

However, the War Office was amazed to discover that the incidence of head injuries increased. It can be assumed that the intensity of fighting was the same before and after the change.

So why should the recorded number of head injuries per battalion increase when the men wore metal helmets instead of cloth caps?

Allow 10-15 minutes and then go around the group asking delegates to read out their answers or conclusion.

You might choose to provide short yes or no answers to delegates questions, although be careful not to lead them too quickly to the

answer. Encourage delegates to explore all possible options, thinking as laterally and creatively as possible.

As an alternative format, delegates can work on the problem in syndicates, creating more of a group interaction and team-building exercise.

The Clues

Q: Did the men wear the helmets?

A: Yes.

Q: When they wore the helmets, did the incidence of head injuries increase?

A: Yes.

Q: And yet they were retained

A: Yes.

Q: Were they beneficial?

A: Yes.

The Answer:

The number of recorded head injuries increased, but the number of deaths decreased. Previously, if a soldier had been hit on the head with a piece of shrapnel it would have pierced his cap and killed him. This would have been recorded as a death, not a head injury. After helmets were issued it was more likely that a piece of shrapnel would cause an injury, not a death. Thus, the incidence of head injuries increased, and the number of deaths decreased.

KING GEORGE IV

Format:	*Pairs/Individual*
Type:	*Climate changer/Energiser*
Time:	*10-15 minutes or as required*
Resources:	*OHP , flip-chart, training resource ref: 115*
Suitable for:	*All levels*

Purpose

To practise creative and lateral thinking.

Procedure

Ask delegates to work in pairs on this exercise, which will test their lateral thinking ability and creativity.

Either read out the story, display as an OHP or distribute as a handout.

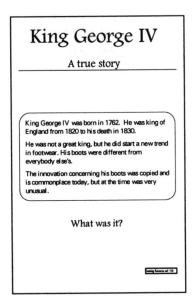

Allow 10-15 minutes and then go around the group asking delegates to read out their answers or conclusion.

You might choose to provide short yes or no answers to delegates questions, although be careful not to lead them too quickly to the

---

answer. Encourage delegates to explore all possible options, thinking as laterally and creatively as possible.

As an alternative format, delegates can work on the problem in syndicates, creating more of a group interaction and team-building exercise.

The clues

What was new about King George's footwear had nothing to do with the following:

- ✓ buckles
- ✓ laces
- ✓ tongues
- ✓ heels
- ✓ soles
- ✓ colour
- ✓ material

It was much more fundamental.

The Answer:

He had a right boot and a left boot! Up until that time all boots had been made to fit on both left and right feet.

THE DREAM

Format:	*Pairs/Individual*
Type:	*Climate change/Energiser*
Time:	*10-15 minutes or as required*
Resources:	*OHP , flip-chart, training resource ref: 116*
Suitable for:	*All levels*

Purpose

To practise creative and lateral thinking.

Procedure

Ask delegates to work in pairs on this exercise, which will test their lateral thinking ability and creativity.

Either read out the story, display as an OHP or distribute as a handout.

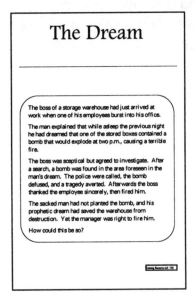

The Dream

The boss of a storage warehouse had just arrived at work when one of his employees burst into his office.

The man explained that while asleep the previous night he had dreamed that one of the stored boxes contained a bomb that would explode at two p.m., causing a terrible fire.

The boss was sceptical but agreed to investigate. After a search, a bomb was found in the area foreseen in the man's dream. The police were called, the bomb defused, and a tragedy averted. Afterwards the boss thanked the employee sincerely, then fired him.

The sacked man had not planted the bomb, and his prophetic dream had saved the warehouse from destruction. Yet the manager was right to fire him.

How could this be so?

Training Resource ref: 116

Allow 10-15 minutes and then go around the group asking delegates to read out their answers or conclusion.

You might choose to provide short yes or no answers to delegates questions, although be careful not to lead them too quickly to the

answer. Encourage delegates to explore all possible options, thinking as laterally and creatively as possible.

As an alternative format, delegates can work on the problem in syndicates, creating more of a group interaction and team-building exercise.

The Clues

Q: Was the man fired because he had had anything to do with   the planting of the bomb?

A: No.

Q: Did the man genuinely dream about the bomb?

A: Yes.

Q: Did the boss have some kind of grudge against the man?

A: No.

Q: Were the man's particular responsibilities relevant?

A: Yes.

The Answer:

The sacked employee was the warehouse night watchman. He should have been awake all night on his security duties. Having a dream proved that he was asleep on the job. For this, he was fired.

THE MAN IN THE HOTEL

Format:	Pairs/Individual
Type:	Climate changer/Energiser
Time:	10-15 minutes or as required
Resources:	OHP, flip-chart, training resource ref: 117
Suitable for:	All levels

Purpose

To practise creative and lateral thinking.

Procedure

Ask delegates to work in pairs on this exercise, which will test their lateral thinking ability and creativity.

Either read out the story, display as an OHP or distribute as a handout.

The Man in the Hotel

Mr Smith and Mr Jones are two businessmen who book into the same hotel for the night.

They are given adjacent rooms on the third floor. During the night, Mr Smith sleeps soundly. However, despite being very tired, Mr Jones can't fall asleep. He eventually phones Mr Smith and falls asleep immediately after hanging up.

Why should this be so?

Allow 10-15 minutes and then go around the group asking delegates to read out their answers or conclusion.

You might choose to provide short yes or no answers to delegates questions, although be careful not to lead them too quickly to the answer. Encourage delegates to explore all possible options, thinking as laterally and creatively as possible.

As an alternative format, delegates can work on the problem in syndicates, creating more of a group interaction and team-building exercise.

The Clues

Q: Was there something happening in Mr Smith's room that was preventing Mr Jones from sleeping?

A: Yes.

Q: Was it a noise?

A: Yes.

Q: Did they speak for long on the phone?

A: No.

The Answer:

Mr Jones could not sleep because Mr Smith was snoring. His phone call awoke Mr Smith and stopped him snoring long enough for Mr Jones to get to sleep.

SHORT ROADS

Format:	Pairs/Individual
Type:	Climate changer/Energiser
Time:	10-15 minutes or as required
Resources:	OHP, flip-chart, training resource ref: 118
Suitable for:	All levels

Purpose

To practise creative and lateral thinking.

Procedure

Ask delegates to work in pairs on this exercise, which will test their lateral thinking ability and creativity.

Either read out the story, display it as an OHP or distribute it as a handout.

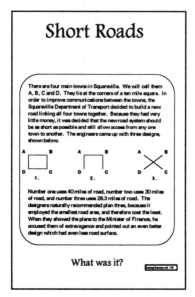

Allow 10-15 minutes and then go around the group asking delegates to read out their answers or conclusion.

You might choose to provide short yes or no answers to delegates questions, although be careful not to lead them too quickly to the

answer. Encourage delegates to explore all possible options, thinking as laterally and creatively as possible.

As alternative format, delegates can work on the problem in syndicates, creating more of a group interaction and team-building exercise.

The Clues

It is hard to believe that a solution exists that requires less road than number 3, however the minister was quite correct. There is a solution which links all four towns with less total road. There are no tricks or corny catches involved.

The Answer:

The shortest distance is shown. It represents 27.3 miles of road and therefore saves a mile in road building expense compared to the two diagonals. Someone starting from A would have a shorter journey to D, but a longer journey to B or C.

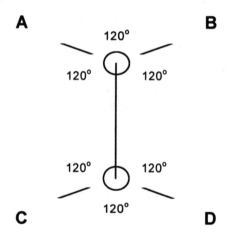

THE PLANE HIJACKER

Format:	Pairs/Individual
Type:	Climate changer/Energiser
Time:	10-15 minutes or as required
Resources:	OHP, flip-chart, training resource ref: 119
Suitable for:	All levels

Purpose

To practise creative and lateral thinking.

Procedure

Ask delegates to work in pairs on this exercise, which will test their lateral thinking ability and creativity.

Either read out the story, display it as an OHP or distribute it as a handout.

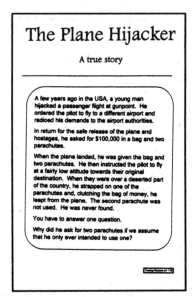

The Plane Hijacker

A true story

A few years ago in the USA, a young man hijacked a passenger flight at gunpoint. He ordered the pilot to fly to a different airport and radioed his demands to the airport authorities.

In return for the safe release of the plane and hostages, he asked for $100,000 in a bag and two parachutes.

When the plane landed, he was given the bag and two parachutes. He then instructed the pilot to fly at a fairly low altitude towards their original destination. When they were over a deserted part of the country, he strapped on one of the parachutes and, clutching the bag of money, he leapt from the plane. The second parachute was not used. He was never found.

You have to answer one question.

Why did he ask for two parachutes if we assume that he only ever intended to use one?

Allow 10-15 minutes and then go around the group asking delegates to read out their answers or conclusion.

You might choose to provide short yes or no answers to delegates questions, although be careful not to lead them too quickly to the answer. Encourage delegates to explore all possible options, thinking as laterally and creatively as possible.

As alternative format, delegates can work on the problem in syndicates, creating more of a group interaction and team-building exercise.

The Clues

Q: Did the man change his mind during the flight?

A: No.

Q: So he had always intended to leap out of the plane on his own?

A: Yes.

Q: Did he carefully choose one parachute in preference to the other?

A: No.

Q: Did he ask for two parachutes in order to deceive the authorities?

A: Yes.

The Answer:

The hijacker asked for two parachutes to make the authorities think he was going to take a hostage with him. They therefore gave him two good parachutes. Had he ask for only one, they would have given him a dud. By asking for two he eliminated that risk. Once he knew that he had two good parachutes, either would do for his escape.

NOTES

NOTES

Appendix

Appendix

Letter Progression

A   E F   H I

   B C D   G   J

What's next?

Reproduced from **Brain-Teasers for Trainers** by Graham Roberts-Phelps and Anne McDougall, Gower, Aldershot.

Spot the
Difference

Working individually, look at the four shapes
below and see if you can find any difference

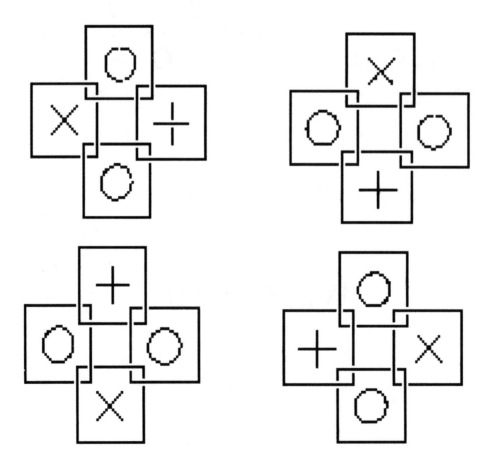

Spot the Difference

Working individually, look at the four shapes below and see if you can find any difference

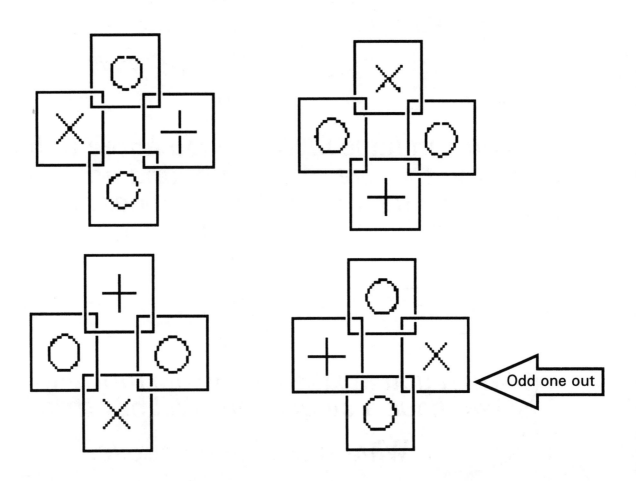

Odd one out

Heads or Tails?

You are walking on a beach and notice an ornate bottle half buried in the sand.

As you pick up and open the bottle a mist rises and materialises into a magical being: a genie. Unlike most genies, this one doesn't give three wishes, he grants three choices.

One

You can have five years added to your life on the condition that another person, selected at random, loses five years of his or her life. Would you take the extra time?

Two

You can have £20,000 if you agree to have a tattoo the size of a five pound note. Would you take the money? If so, where would you place the tattoo and what design would you choose?

Three

When you awake tomorrow morning you can have a single new skill or attribute.

What would you choose?

Training Resource ref: 3

Reproduced from **Brain-Teasers for Trainers** by Graham Roberts-Phelps and Anne McDougall, Gower, Aldershot.

Sprouts

Mathematician John Conway developed a fascinating and easy-to-learn game called Sprouts. The playing surface is a group of sixteen dots arranged in a four by four grid. Two players alternate moves by connecting any two dots together with a straight or curved line. A new dot is placed on this line. Lines cannot intersect and a dot may have at most three lines connected to it. The aim of the game is to have the last move.

0   0   0   0

0   0   0   0

0   0   0   0

0   0   0   0

Reproduced from **Brain-Teasers for Trainers** by Graham Roberts-Phelps and Anne McDougall, Gower, Aldershot.

Exercising Your Visual Memory

Look at the following figures for a minute, then draw them as accurately as you can from memory.

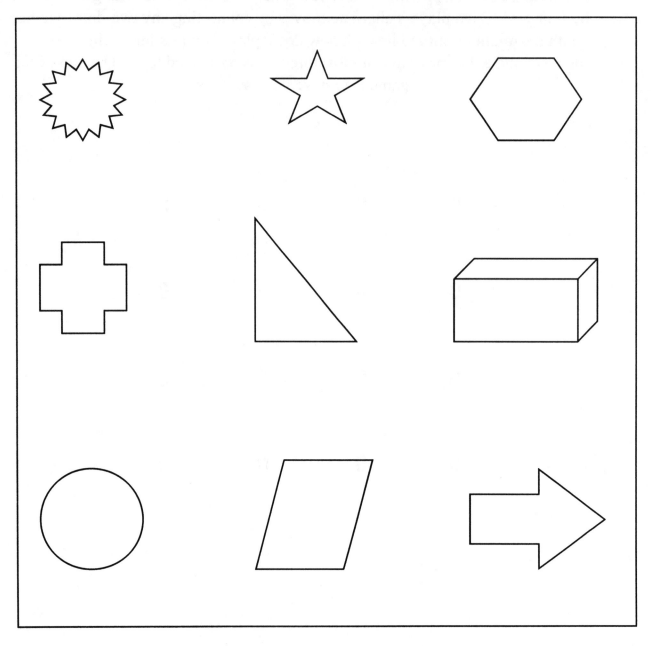

Training Resource ref: 5

Exercising Your Visual Memory

Look at the following figures for a minute, then draw them as accurately as you can from memory.

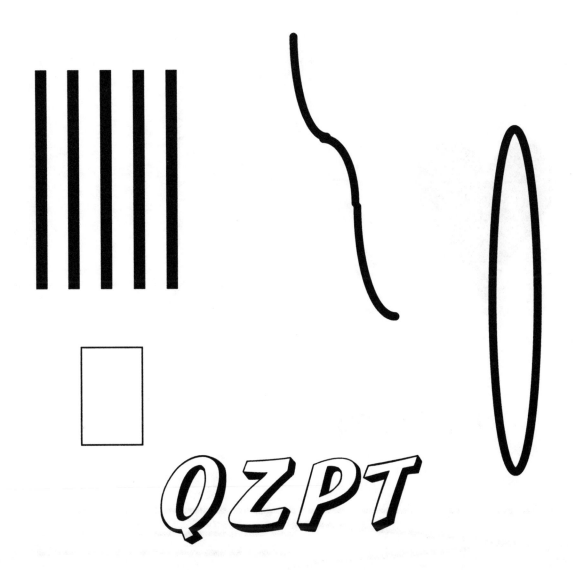

Reproduced from **Brain-Teasers for Trainers** by Graham Roberts-Phelps and Anne McDougall, Gower, Aldershot.

Exercising Your Visual Memory

Look at the following figures for a minute, then draw them as accurately as you can from memory.

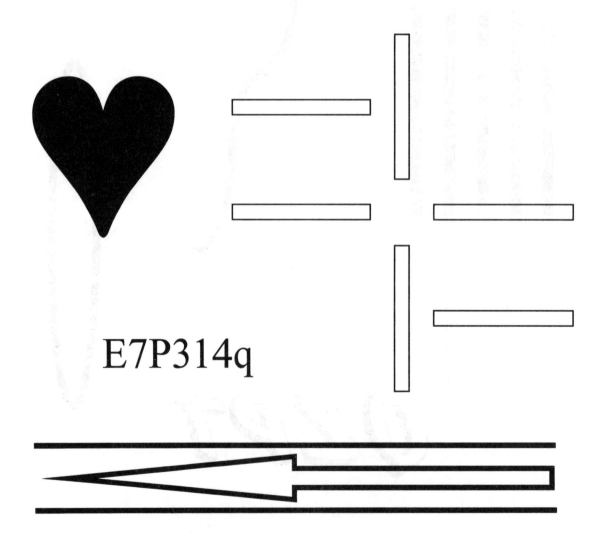

E7P314q

Reproduced from **Brain-Teasers for Trainers** by Graham Roberts-Phelps and Anne McDougall, Gower, Aldershot.

Exercising Your Visual Memory

Look at the following figures for a minute, then draw them as accurately as you can from memory.

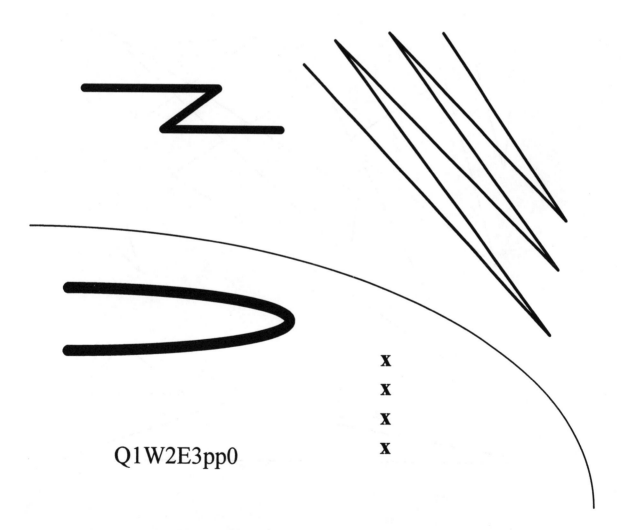

Q1W2E3pp0

Reproduced from **Brain-Teasers for Trainers** by Graham Roberts-Phelps and Anne McDougall, Gower, Aldershot.

Exercising Your Visual Memory

Look at the following figures for a minute, then draw them as accurately as you can from memory.

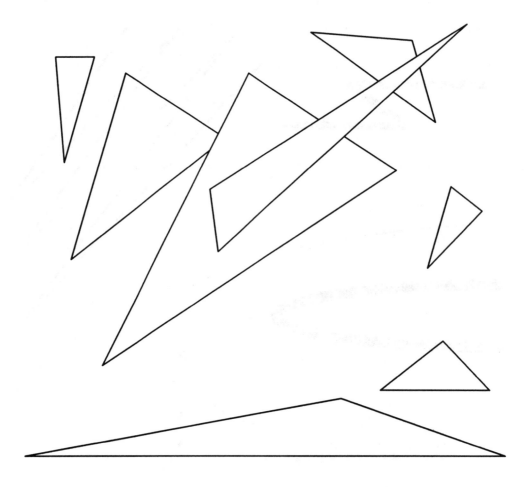

Reproduced from **Brain-Teasers for Trainers** by Graham Roberts-Phelps and Anne McDougall, Gower, Aldershot.

Thinking as Sequencing

One aspect of problem solving and analysis is how we divide up a large, complex plan of action into a series of simpler actions. For example, select three of the following and write out the steps you need to perform to achieve these projects. List possible alternatives if things don't go according to plan.

✓ Making your first million

✓ Training and keeping a pet monkey

✓ Travelling to China on a bicycle

✓ Learning competition-level tennis

✓ Becoming fluent in a foreign language

✓ Becoming a clothes designer for a rock band

✓ Building an extension to your home

✓ Building your own home

✓ Rewiring your house or flat

✓ Putting a new bathroom in your house

✓ Going on holiday or an overseas trip

✓ Starting a newspaper

✓ Designing a restaurant

Training Resource ref: 10

Reproduced from **Brain-Teasers for Trainers** by Graham Roberts-Phelps and Anne McDougall, Gower, Aldershot.

Nine Dots

Connect the nine dots below using only four straight lines, without taking your pen off the paper.

0   0   0

0   0   0

0   0   0

Training Resource ref: 11

Nine Dots

Connect the nine dots below using only four straight lines, without taking your pen off the paper.

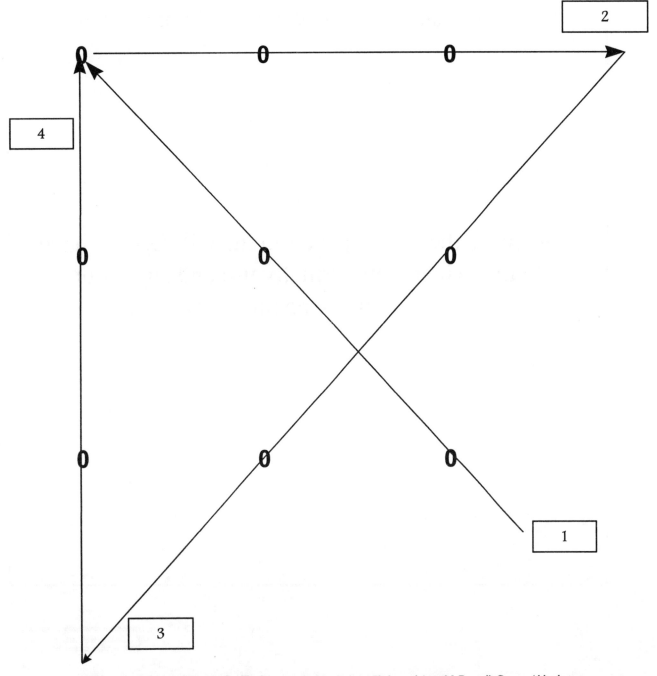

Force of Habit

Please complete the following:

Sign your name here as you would normally do:

Now place the pen or pencil in the OPPOSITE hand to that which you normally use and sign your name again.

Training Resource ref: 12

PARIS IN
IN THE SPRING

Reproduced from **Brain-Teasers for Trainers** by Graham Roberts-Phelps and Anne McDougall, Gower, Aldershot.

Paragraph Puzzler

'George looked out over the fields, only to see three young children climbing the hedge into the sheep's pen. "Oi!" he yelled loudly. "Get yourselves out of there!" But his shouts went unnoticed by the children. Jumping down from his jeep, he set off over the muddy field in the direction of the sheep.
While the ploughed field would be tricky for most people to run on, he quickly got to the hedge next to the sheep. His sudden presence rooted the children to the spot in surprise. "Hey you kids, you'll frighten them sheep, now get out of there!" Without further thought, they took to their heels, not stopping until they got to the next field.'

Question: *What is unusual about this passage?*

Reproduced from **Brain-Teasers for Trainers** by Graham Roberts-Phelps and Anne McDougall, Gower, Aldershot.

Swot analysis

Strengths	Weaknesses
Opportunities	Threats

Reproduced from **Brain-Teasers for Trainers** by Graham Roberts-Phelps and Anne McDougall, Gower, Aldershot.

Numeric Progression/1

Working in groups of two or three, continue the progression and find a way to explain this. After five minutes elect one delegate to present your solution to the rest of the group.

3 1 2 8 3 1 3 0 . . .

Training Resource ref: 16

Numeric Progression/2

Working individually, explain which number is the odd one out of the sequence and why.

4   29   42   68

Reproduced from **Brain-Teasers for Trainers** by Graham Roberts-Phelps and Anne McDougall, Gower, Aldershot.

Number Jumble

Read each of the following series of numbers to yourself.
After each series, close your eyes, and repeat the numbers
or write them down.

Which is the longest series you can hold in your mind?

3 5 4 8 4

5 7 9 1 3 2

2 5 4 7 7 0 4

8 5 7 1 3 2 7 0

2 4 6 5 8 4 2 4 5

1 2 6 1 9 4 1 7 2 1 1 9 6 9

Reproduced from **Brain-Teasers for Trainers** by Graham Roberts-Phelps and Anne McDougall, Gower, Aldershot.

Mental Staying Power / 1

In your head, count the number of capital letters of the alphabet that contain curved lines.

Start now.

Training Resource ref: 19

Mental Staying Power/2

Once upon a time in ancient Rome, a peasant farmer saved the life of the son of a very wealthy landowner during a dispute over a local matter. In gratitude, the wealthy man offered the peasant any reward he could name. The farmer replied that he would like the landowner to place a one- penny piece on a chess board, and then have it doubled for every square on the board. The landowner roared with laughter at the simpleton's ridiculous request and agreed straight away. But was this as daft as it sounds?

How much did the farmer receive from the man?

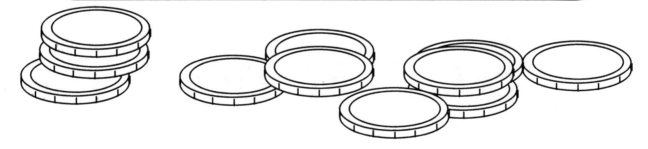

Performing the calculation in their heads. You may keep a tally of boxes or doubles completed.

Training Resource ref: 20

Prestidigitation 100

There is a popular number puzzle in which you must use all the digits from one to nine and any combination of plus signs and minus signs to add up to 100.

Task 1:
Find a solution, working as quickly as possible.

Task 2:
Find another solution that uses only three signs.

1 – 2 – 3 – 4 – 5 – 6 – 7 – 8 – 9 – 10

Training Resource ref: 21

Reproduced from **Brain-Teasers for Trainers** by Graham Roberts-Phelps and Anne McDougall, Gower, Aldershot.

Language and Meaning

Give your definition of the following words or phrases.

What do they mean to you?

How might others understand them?

- ⊠ Annoying
- ⊠ Relax!
- ⊠ No problem!
- ⊠ I won't be a minute
- ⊠ Unfortunately..
- ⊠ With due respect..
- ⊠ Off the record..
- ⊠ I would be grateful if you could.
- ⊠ Can I help you?
- ⊠ Have a nice day.?
- ⊠ To be honest.!
- ⊠ We're looking into it.
- ⊠ That's an interesting point
- ⊠ I'll be in touch
- ⊠ We must have lunch sometime
- ⊠ I have instructed to tell...
- ⊠ The cheque's in the post

Training Resource ref: 22

Reproduced from **Brain-Teasers for Trainers** by Graham Roberts-Phelps and Anne McDougall, Gower, Aldershot.

Lie Detector Test

HANDOUT FOR 'SUSPECT'

Take a few moments to prepare your answers to the following questions. You will be interviewed twice regarding your activities and whereabouts last weekend. At one interview you will be completely and absolutely truthful, at the other you will be completely untruthful (you can decide which). Your goal is to mislead the group into believing the false account - only you will know which one, tell no one else.

Interview questions you may be asked

What did you do last weekend?

- **Give a detailed and timed breakdown of your movements and activities.**
- **Who did you meet?**
- **Where did you go?**
- **Who did you speak to?**
- **Did you enjoy it?**
- **Was it a good weekend?**
- **Your thoughts about it.**

Training Resource ref: 23

Reproduced from **Brain-Teasers for Trainers** by Graham Roberts-Phelps and Anne McDougall, Gower, Aldershot.

Lie Detector Test

OBSERVER'S SHEET

> Please make notes in the spaces provided during the interview. Leave your conclusions until you have seen both interviews.

Suspect name_____

Interview A	Interview B

This suspect was lying on interview _____

Suspect name_____

Interview A	Interview B

This suspect was lying on interview _____

Suspect name_____

Interview A	Interview B

This suspect was lying on interview _____

Training Resource ref: 24

Reproduced from **Brain-Teasers for Trainers** by Graham Roberts-Phelps and Anne McDougall, Gower, Aldershot.

Course "Rules"

1. Have fun - create energy

2. Create choices wherever possible

3. With risk comes reward

4. We learn best by doing

5. We are learning for real life

6. Take responsibility for your own learning

Training Resource ref: 25

Training Course Rules

1. **Have fun - create energy**

   Enjoy the course, approach it positively with a good sense of humour and contribute actively.

2. **Create choices wherever possible**

   It is not intended to create 'clones' where everybody says and does the same things. Nor is 'perfection' a goal. The purpose of the training is to create more and better choices when selling, leading to greater success.

3. **With risk comes reward**

   Try different things and experiment. A training course is a safe environment in which to learn and try out new skills and techniques. While there is a risk of failure, there is always reward and benefit.

4. **Learn best by doing**

   Just as you cannot learn to swim by reading about it, you learn and develop customer service and quality skills by doing them.

5. **We are learning for real life**

   While a classroom situation is artificial and role plays are by definition simulations, the purpose of the course is to achieve measurable improvements in real life.

6. **Take responsibility for your own learning**

   Take notes, ask questions, challenge things you don't understand, agree nobody can teach you anything, only help you to learn.

Training Resource ref: 26

Reproduced from **Brain-Teasers for Trainers** by Graham Roberts-Phelps and Anne McDougall, Gower, Aldershot.

One~Way Communication

Describe the following shapes to someone who cannot see them. Have that person draw a picture of the shapes from your description.

Training Resource ref: 27

Self~Assessment Questions/1

1. **Briefly, how do you view your role in your current position?**

2. **If you could have any position or job you wanted, what would you do?**

3. **What qualities do you feel you have that are most valuable to the company?**

4. **What qualities do you have that you feel are currently underused?**

5. **If you could live your life again, what changes would you make?**

Training Resource ref: 28

Reproduced from **Brain-Teasers for Trainers** by Graham Roberts-Phelps and Anne McDougall, Gower, Aldershot.

Self~Assessment Questions/2

1. **What do you think makes the difference between success and failure in your business or profession?**

2. **What do you feel has been your greatest accomplishment in your life?**

3. **What has been your greatest disappointment?**

4. **What have you done in the past year to improve yourself?**

5. **How do you visualise your future?**

Training Resource ref: 29

Reproduced from **Brain-Teasers for Trainers** by Graham Roberts-Phelps and Anne McDougall, Gower, Aldershot.

Self~Assessment Questions/3

1. How important is money to you?

2. How does your spouse feel about your job and how interested are they in the company?

3. What are your pet hates, the things that upset you the most?

4. What do most people often criticise you for?

5. What do you most often criticise others for?

Reproduced from **Brain-Teasers for Trainers** by Graham Roberts-Phelps and Anne McDougall, Gower, Aldershot.

Self~Assessment Questions/4

1. What factors in your past have contributed most to your own development?

2. What factors in your past have been handicaps in preventing you from moving ahead more quickly?

3. Who do you consider to be the most successful person you have ever met?

   Why?

4. Describe your life and the things around as you would like them to be in ten years' time.

5. What really motivates you?

Reproduced from **Brain-Teasers for Trainers** by Graham Roberts-Phelps and Anne McDougall, Gower, Aldershot.

Instant Persuasion

You have three minutes to persuade another group member to do something which would be good for him or her (e.g. miss lunch, lose weight, take up aerobics, read a certain book, watch less television). Use a high-pressure style. The other person may resist and, if persuaded, must actually carry out the action to which he or she agreed. Take a few minutes to collect your thoughts and make some notes:

Objective:

Notes:

Reproduced from **Brain-Teasers for Trainers** by Graham Roberts-Phelps and Anne McDougall, Gower, Aldershot.

Making Sense of Words

Take some everyday expressions and practise making them mean different things. For instance, see if can you say '*Good morning*' to communicate:

Anger	**Enthusiasm**
Annoyance	**Friendliness**
Authority	**Happiness**
Cheerfulness	**Impatience**
Confidence	**Indifference**
Delight	**Joy**
Depression	**Patronising**
Energy	**Sadness**

Training Resource ref: 33

Reproduced from **Brain-Teasers for Trainers** by Graham Roberts-Phelps and Anne McDougall, Gower, Aldershot.

Points of View

Identify a topic that you feel strongly about and write your views on this in the space below.

For example, smoking, blood sports, bad customer service etc ...

Topic/your feeling about this is:

Training Resource ref: 34

Get It Off Your Chest!

Identify a specific authority figure in your life (parent, teacher, present or former boss) who has not treated you as you would expect to be treated.

Choose a group member to play the role of this person and tell him or her how you are to be treated from now on. **Demand specific changes in his or her behaviour.** *The authority figure may respond.*

Reproduced from **Brain-Teasers for Trainers** by Graham Roberts-Phelps and Anne McDougall, Gower, Aldershot.

How Well Do You Listen?

Read the following passage to delegates:

Health and Safety At Work Act 1974

This piece of legislation was enacted in 1974, as the name suggests. It was brought in to replace and update much of the old Health and Safety law which was contained in the **Factories Act of 1961 and the Offices, Shops and Railway Premises Act of 1963.** These two pieces of legislation were fast becoming out of date with modern working practices, technology and equipment. Here are some UK accident statistics produced by the Health and Safety Executive for 1994:

1.6 million injury accidents of which 640,000 resulted in absences of 3 days or more

2.2 million people suffering ill-health caused or made worse by work

27 million non-injury accidents

30 million working days lost1

18 million through accidents

11.6 million through ill-health.

There are more working days lost through accidents and ill-health than are ever lost through industrial disputes.

Here are some key points raised by the Act.

1. Safeguards

Employers are required to implement reasonable safeguards to ensure safe working practise at all times. This means taking every practical step to remove hazards and reduce or eliminate risks. The law interprets this as taking every possible precaution, and **cost is not considered as an excuse for failure to do this**.

2. Written policy

All organisations employing five or more people must have a written and up-to-date health and safety policy. They must also carry out written risk assessments as part of the implementation of their safety policy. They must also **display a current certificate as required by the Employer's Liability Act**.

3. Training and information

Following from this all staff must be fully trained, equipped and informed of not only the company's safety policy and procedures, but also of the skills and knowledge necessary to carry out their normal work duties. This of course means **displaying Health and Safety regulations and safety signs**, as well as formally training and directing staff on all aspects of health, safety, hazards and risks.

4. Reasonable care

Of course, the legislation does not just cover employers and organisations, there are definite requirements placed on employees. All employees must take reasonable care and follow all procedures fully. Failure to do so is in breach of the Act.

5. Safe systems of work

Employers must also ensure what are called 'safe systems of work', which means creating an environment that is conducive to health and safety. This can be as basic as making sure that buildings are in good repair, that proper heat and ventilation are provided, and the workplace is clean and hygienic to work in.

Training Resource ref: 36

How Well Do You Listen?

Questions

Health and Safety At Work Act 1974

1. When was the Health and Safety At Work Act introduced?

2. Which two pieces of legislation did it replace?

3. What are the five main sections or areas it covers?

4. What size of companies are covered by the Act?

5. What must an employer display?

6. What is not considered an excuse for failing to provide safety equipment or standards?

7. What main requirements are placed on employees as a result of the Act?

8. How many working days were lost in 1994 through accident, job-related illness or injury?

9. How many accidents occurred in the UK?

10. How many resulted in absences of three or more days?

Training Resource ref: 37

Reproduced from **Brain-Teasers for Trainers** by Graham Roberts-Phelps and Anne McDougall, Gower, Aldershot.

A Letter to Myself

Name and address:

_____

_____

_____

_____

Date: _____

Dear me,

After my course today, I will begin to be more effective in the following areas:

Changes and action   by date:

_____

1.

2.

3.

4.

5.

_____

Best wishes and well done!

Yours sincerely,

Reproduced from **Brain-Teasers for Trainers** by Graham Roberts-Phelps and Anne McDougall, Gower, Aldershot.

This Is Me!

> Working in pairs, please complete the following statements and answer the questions. Discuss your responses before moving on to the next question.

1. If I walked into a bookshop and purchased a book for leisure reading, the title would probably be ...

2. If I stopped to listen to a 'soap box' speaker, the subject of his or her speech might be ...

3. Reading the daily newspaper, I notice an article that makes me angry. It is probably about ...

4. My favourite humorous TV show is ...   Because?...

5. A serious TV programmes I really enjoy is ...

6. The last film I really enjoyed was ... Because? ...

7. My favourite film of all time is probably? ...

8. The last time I went to a party was ...   Did you enjoy it?

9. When I listen to the radio it is ... When and which station?

10. I belong to the following groups and associations ...

11. People who know me best think I'm ...

12. At a party or social gathering, my behaviour could best be described as ...

13. I would say my greatest communication strength is ...

14. I would say my greatest communication weakness is ...

15. Working with other people makes me feel ...

16. I relax by ...

17. The one thing that I would like to change about myself is ...

18. I prefer to work and spend time with people who ...

Reproduced from **Brain-Teasers for Trainers** by Graham Roberts-Phelps and Anne McDougall, Gower, Aldershot.

Coat of Arms

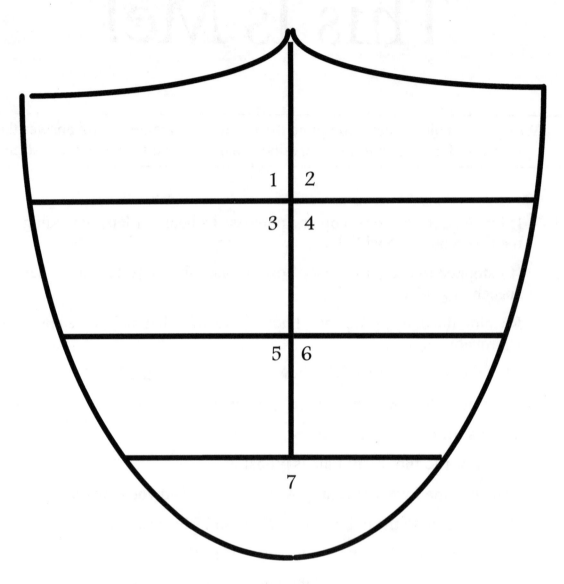

- In section 1, list two things you do very well.

- In section 2, write your personal maxim or motto.

- In section 3, list what you consider to be your greatest achievement in life.

- In section 4, list the three individuals who have influenced you most.

- In section 5, list the three things about you that you consider to be most important.

- In section 6, list the two major goals you have for the next two years.

- In section 7, list the one place you most enjoy being.

First Day at Work

What was your
first full-time
job?

Recall your first
day in this job.

What advice
would you give
to someone just
starting their
first day at
work?

Training Resource ref: 41

Personal Strengths

Make some notes in answer to the following questions, and then present these when asked.

1. What natural abilities do I have?

2. What things do I do better than most people?

3. How have I grown in the last year?

4. What are the most difficult things I have accomplished?

5. What am I proudest of?

6. On what would I most like to receive compliments about myself?

Reproduced from **Brain-Teasers for Trainers** by Graham Roberts-Phelps and Anne McDougall, Gower, Aldershot.

Personal Weaknesses

Make some notes in answer to the following questions, and then present these when asked.

1. What about me most upsets the people I work with?

2. What criticism would my closest friend give me if asked?

3. What am I least proud of?

4. What criticism would my boss give me?

5. What area(s) of my behaviour would I most like to improve?

Training Resource ref: 43

Reproduced from **Brain-Teasers for Trainers** by Graham Roberts-Phelps and Anne McDougall, Gower, Aldershot.

Six Questions

Please answer the following questions as quickly as possible, writing your first few, intuitive responses.

1. What would you do if you won £1million on the lottery next week?

2. What would you do if you only had six months to live?

3. What do you dream of achieving, attempting or experiencing?

4. What is your greatest fear that holds you back?

5. Describe your ideal job or working situation.

6. What one great thing would you dare to dream if you knew you couldn't fail?

Training Resource ref: 44

Reproduced from **Brain-Teasers for Trainers** by Graham Roberts-Phelps and Anne McDougall, Gower, Aldershot.

How Assertive Are You?

Working in small groups, consider each of the three situations in turn and discuss how you would react and what you would do.

1 It is a busy Saturday morning and you are out shopping. You are just about to move into a parking space when a sports car comes from nowhere and takes your space. What do you do?

2 A colleague asks you to do some work which you feel they should really be doing themselves. You have too much to do as it is.

3 You are standing in a queue of about eight people at the cash machine outside your local bank. A little old lady pushes in right at the front, without asking and takes the next turn. What would you do? Would this change if a different person pushed in?

Training Resource ref: 45

Reproduced from **Brain-Teasers for Trainers** by Graham Roberts-Phelps and Anne McDougall, Gower, Aldershot.

How Do You Solve Problems?

Working in a small group, discuss the following points,
identifying at least one example each.

1   Can you give an example of one of the most
difficult decisions that you ever had to make?

2.   Can you give an example of a decision that was
easy?

3.   Can you give an example of a decision that
turned out to be a mistake?

4.   How do you weigh options when making BIG
decisions?

5.   What is your approach when making small
everyday decisions, such as what to do at the
weekend?

Training Resource ref: 46

Reproduced from **Brain-Teasers for Trainers** by Graham Roberts-Phelps and Anne McDougall, Gower, Aldershot.

Prisoner's Dilemma

Following the collapse of your company due to massive financial irregularities, the Serious Fraud Office has arrested you and one of your colleagues on suspicion of fraud and embezzlement. In order to avoid lengthy and expensive court proceedings, they have given you both the following option:

You can plead guilty and take full responsibility for the crime, or plead not guilty and deny any involvement or knowledge. If you both confess, you will both automatically be sentenced to ten years in jail and a million pound fine. If you confess but your colleague does not, you will be set free, after giving evidence to convict your partner and returning all the money. He or she will then serve a non-negotiable ten-year jail term and a million pound fine. If you do not confess, but he or she does, you will receive the jail term and fine, and he or she will go free. If neither of you confesses, you will both be convicted of complicity and sentenced to a five-year jail sentence and enforced bankruptcy.

You have five minutes to decide how to plead.

Reproduced from **Brain-Teasers for Trainers** by Graham Roberts-Phelps and Anne McDougall, Gower, Aldershot.

Personal Preferences

Please complete the following statements, giving your first or instinctive answer:

1. **At school my favourite subject was:**

2. **My favourite meal or food is:**

3. **My favourite record/CD that I own is:**

4. **My favourite outfit or piece of clothing is:**

5. **My favourite drink is:**

6. **The best holiday I ever had was spent in:**

7. **My favourite film of all time is:**

8. **My favourite television programme at the moment is:**

9. **I prefer to read the following daily newspaper:**

10. **My preferred radio station is:**

11. **My most prized possession is my:**

12. **My favourite leisure time activity is:**

Reproduced from **Brain-Teasers for Trainers** by Graham Roberts-Phelps and Anne McDougall, Gower, Aldershot.

Right to Strike

You are the Human Resources committee of the Government Personnel Advisory Board. You have been asked to present some guidelines regarding the right to strike and take industrial action for various occupations. As an election is on the horizon, you must make your choices very carefully, and make sure you can justify your recommendations.

Discuss within your group and rank the following occupational groups with 1 for the group with the most right to strike down to 19 for the group with the least right to strike.

Rank these occupations:
- **Airline staff**
- **Bus drivers**
- **Civil servants (tax, customs & excise, etc ...)**
- **Construction workers**
- **Doctors**
- **Farm labourers and workers**
- **Firecrew**
- **Hairdressers**
- **Nurses**
- **Oil field workers and coal miners**
- **Police**
- **Politicians**
- **Rail staff**
- **Refuse collectors**
- **Retail, customer service and sales staff**
- **Teachers**
- **Telephone engineers**
- **Television presenters and staff**
- **Truck drivers**

Training Resource ref: 49

Reproduced from **Brain-Teasers for Trainers** by Graham Roberts-Phelps and Anne McDougall, Gower, Aldershot.

The Photocopy Machine

'The photocopy machine broke down in your office this morning and has only just been repaired. It is now 4:00 PM and by 8:30am tomorrow, 150 folders have to be filled with 20 pages of material for a conference. It is your job as a manager to tell your assistant that he or she must stay late and do all the photocopying. You happen to know that your subordinate has tickets for a popular concert tonight, for which he or she stood in line for hours and to which they have been looking forward for weeks.'

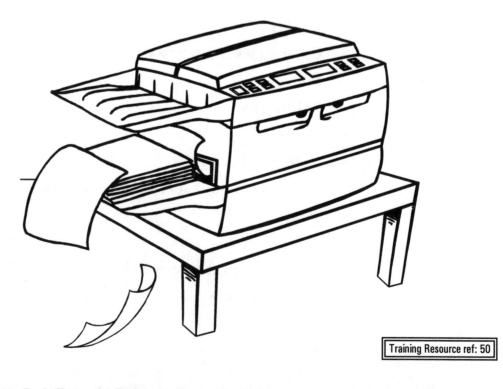

Training Resource ref: 50

Reproduced from **Brain-Teasers for Trainers** by Graham Roberts-Phelps and Anne McDougall, Gower, Aldershot.

Warm~up Game

TAKE 5-10 MINUTES TO DESIGN A 5-10 MINUTE WARM-UP EXERCISE THAT YOU CAN RUN IN 5-10 MINUTES' TIME.

Reproduced from **Brain-Teasers for Trainers** by Graham Roberts-Phelps and Anne McDougall, Gower, Aldershot.

Word Bluff

Introduction for delegates

The purpose of the exercise is to 'bluff' the other teams or group members into believing that an incorrect meaning rather than the real meaning of the word is correct.

Each team of three takes it in turns to present their word (write this on the flip-chart), and their three proposed definitions (one per person). You must make the two false meanings sound as believable as possible.

After all three versions have been presented, the other teams or audience vote for the definition they believe to be correct. The one with the most votes is taken as the answer.

The trainer then reveals whether the others are correct or not and scores two points for correctly bluffing, or deducts two points if they are unsuccessful.

Reproduced from **Brain-Teasers for Trainers** by Graham Roberts-Phelps and Anne McDougall, Gower, Aldershot.

Word Bluff/1

The word is: <u>Dieldrin</u>

Definition 1:
A crystalline substance, consisting of a chlorinated derivative of naphthalene; a contact insecticide.

Definition 2:
The device holding the dies used to cut the external screw thread.

Definition 3:
An ancient Hindu religion, characterized by the belief that the material world is progressing endlessly in a series of cycles.

Training Resource ref: 53

Word Bluff/2

The word is: <u>Pseudepigrapha</u>

Definition 1:
Various Jewish writings from the first century BC to the first century AD that claim to have been divinely revealed but have been excluded from the Old Testament.

Definition 2:
The psychology of all known languages, including language acquisition by children, language disorders, i.e. why people may stutter etc ...

Definition 3:
An ancient stringed instrument similar to the lyre, but having a trapezoidal sounding board over which the strings are stretched.

Training Resource ref: 54

Reproduced from **Brain-Teasers for Trainers** by Graham Roberts-Phelps and Anne McDougall, Gower, Aldershot.

Word Bluff/3

The word is: <u>Damask</u>

Definition 1:
A family of languages, including Tamil and Malayalam, spoken in south and central India and Sri Lanka.

Definition 2:
A cold dish of meat or poultry, which is boned, cooked, then pressed and glazed.

Definition 3:
A reversible fabric, usually silk or linen, with a pattern woven into it. It is used for table linen, curtains etc ...

Reproduced from **Brain-Teasers for Trainers** by Graham Roberts-Phelps and Anne McDougall, Gower, Aldershot.

Word Bluff/4

The word is: <u>Riffle</u>

Definition 1:
A gap or space made by cleaving or splitting, and a fault produced by tension on either side of the fault plane.

Definition 2:
A contrivance on the bottom of a sluice, containing grooves for trapping particles of gold (as in mining).

Definition 3:
Slang word used mainly by black American children meaning to get/steal something that proves your respect and loyalty to a gang or posse.

Reproduced from **Brain-Teasers for Trainers** by Graham Roberts-Phelps and Anne McDougall, Gower, Aldershot.

Word Bluff/5

The word is: <u>Defoliant</u>

Definition 1:
A chemical sprayed or dusted on trees to cause their leaves to fall.

Definition 2:
A subsection of the famous Folio Society book club which is obliged to publish books specifically relating to religious movements.

Definition 3:
A style of architecture and decoration that originated in France in the early eighteenth century, characterised by elaborate but graceful ornamentation.

Reproduced from **Brain-Teasers for Trainers** by Graham Roberts-Phelps and Anne McDougall, Gower, Aldershot.

Word Bluff/6

The word is: <u>Scleroderma</u>

Definition 1:
A light-coloured coarse-grained igneous rock consisting of feldspars and hornblend.

Definition 2:
Something that has both the characteristics and shape of any letter in the Greek alphabet.

Definition 3:
A chronic disease common among women, characterised by thickening and hardening of the skin.

Training Resource ref: 58

Word Bluff/7

The word is : <u>Torticollis</u>

Definition 1:
A vertical glass tube partly evacuated and partly filled with mercury, which is then used to measure atmospheric pressure.

Definition 2:
An abnormal position of the head, which is usually characterised by the bent position of the neck to one side.

Definition 3:
A German sweet which consists of almonds and hazelnuts encased in sugar and served with cherry liqueur.

Reproduced from **Brain-Teasers for Trainers** by Graham Roberts-Phelps and Anne McDougall, Gower, Aldershot.

Word Bluff/8

The word is: <u>Monetarism</u>

Definition 1:
**The theory that inflation is caused by
an excess quantity of money in an
economy.**

Definition 2:
**The study of the life, art and
behaviour of the French landscape
painter Claude Monet, which was
introduced as a topic of study at the
Royal Academy of Art.**

Definition 3:
**The doctrine that reality consists of
only one basic substance or element,
such as mind or matter.**

Reproduced from **Brain-Teasers for Trainers** by Graham Roberts-Phelps and Anne McDougall, Gower, Aldershot.

Word Bluff/9

The word is: <u>Geodesy</u>

Definition 1:
The term used to describe the history and past beliefs of the use of geographical equipment and methods.

Definition 2:
A position of supposed eminence or superiority which was popular with the Roman senates, the term eventually dying out in the third century AD.

Definition 3:
The branch of science concerned with determining the exact positioning of geographical points, and the shape and size of the earth.

Word Bluff/10

The word is: Trireme

Definition 1:
An ancient Greek galley with three banks of oars on each side.

Definition 2:
The state of being when the mouth is unable to open because of sustained contractions of the jaw muscles, caused by tetanus.

Definition 3:
An old expression used by the upper class in the middle to late eighteenth century which means you are very intelligent and philosophical.

Training Resource ref: 62

Three Things In Common

Circulate around the room and introduce yourself to other delegates, ideally those you have not met before, and find at least three other people that you have something in common with.

Reproduced from **Brain-Teasers for Trainers** by Graham Roberts-Phelps and Anne McDougall, Gower, Aldershot.

Challenge Match

Based on everything we have discussed or covered in the previous training course or session, prepare eight challenging questions to ask the other team. Just for the fun of it, add two additional questions about anything at all which have nothing to do with this course. Teams will exchange questions alternately, and you will earn two points for a correct answer, and one bonus point for every incorrect answer by the other team.

Your eight questions:

1.

2.

3.

4.

5.

6.

7.

8.

Reproduced from **Brain-Teasers for Trainers** by Graham Roberts-Phelps and Anne McDougall, Gower, Aldershot.

Consultants Inc

Choose a problem or concern that may prevent you or your team from carrying out your job more effectively, OR from implementing some of the ideas on this course.

SWAP PROBLEMS WITH ANOTHER GROUP

SPEND 20 MINUTES FINDING A SOLUTION

REPORT YOUR SOLUTION TO THE GROUP

Training Resource ref: 65

Wanted Poster

TASK:

You have to design a "Wanted Poster" for a company superstar for your job.
The poster should describe how people would recognise this person, what they would look like, where they might be last seen, and explain just what sort of character he or she is.
It should also say that a large reward is available for anybody helping to find this person.

Reproduced from **Brain-Teasers for Trainers** by Graham Roberts-Phelps and Anne McDougall, Gower, Aldershot.

Brainstorming

To get a few good ideas...

...first generate lots of ideas!

Reproduced from **Brain-Teasers for Trainers** by Graham Roberts-Phelps and Anne McDougall, Gower, Aldershot.

Brain storming
Action Plan

Name: ....

- The five best ideas arising from this session are:
  1.
  2.
  3.
  4.
  5.

- Five things (actions) I will be doing to improve as result of this exercise:
  1.
  2.
  3.
  4.
  5.

- Five things I will NOT be doing (or will stop doing) that will improve as result of this exercise:
  1.
  2.
  3.
  4.
  5.

Training Resource ref: 68

Reproduced from **Brain-Teasers for Trainers** by Graham Roberts-Phelps and Anne McDougall, Gower, Aldershot.

Pirate Raid ~ Team A

As a test of your powers of persuasion, creativity and lateral thinking, collect as many of the items listed in 15 minutes or less. One point will be awarded for every item collected, and one bonus point for every minute under 15 minutes, but only if all items are collected.

- ✔ some foreign currency
- ✔ cheque for £1 million
- ✔ a boiled sweet
- ✔ the name and address of a complete stranger (in their handwriting)
- ✔ a piece of underwear
- ✔ a cooking utensil
- ✔ the price of a Ford Escort
- ✔ a car number plate
- ✔ a toilet roll
- ✔ a coin dated before 1980
- ✔ a £50 note
- ✔ the telephone number of the British Embassy in Paris
- ✔ the full name and date of birth of your managing director

Training Resource ref: 69

Reproduced from **Brain-Teasers for Trainers** by Graham Roberts-Phelps and Anne McDougall, Gower, Aldershot.

Pirate Raid ~ Team B

As a test of your powers of persuasion, creativity and lateral thinking, collect as many of the items listed in 15 minutes or less. One point will be awarded for every item collected, and one bonus point for every minute under 15 minutes, but only if all items are collected.

- ✓ some foreign currency
- ✓ cheque for a £1 million
- ✓ a piece of fruit
- ✓ the name and address of a complete stranger (in their handwriting)
- ✓ a flower
- ✓ a workshop tool
- ✓ the price of a dozen eggs
- ✓ a sign or notice
- ✓ a very old newspaper or magazine
- ✓ a coin dated before 1980
- ✓ a £50 note
- ✓ the telephone number of the French Embassy in London
- ✓ the full name and date of birth of your youngest employee

Training Resource ref: 70

Reproduced from **Brain-Teasers for Trainers** by Graham Roberts-Phelps and Anne McDougall, Gower, Aldershot.

Personal History

Interview the person next to you to find out some personal facts (where they live, age, family etc ...), together with some information about their position now, and also the answer to the following question:

'What are the highlights in your career?'

Reproduced from **Brain-Teasers for Trainers** by Graham Roberts-Phelps and Anne McDougall, Gower, Aldershot.

Precision Problem Solving

The first step towards solving any problem is to figure out what you need to figure out.
In the following puzzle, start off by determining your objective and then restate the puzzle in a way that makes it easier to approach.

> **A zoo in Tallahassee has thirty heads and one hundred feet.**
> **How many beast and how many birds does the zoo contain?**

Reproduced from **Brain-Teasers for Trainers** by Graham Roberts-Phelps and Anne McDougall, Gower, Aldershot.

Precision Problem Solving

The first step towards solving any problem is to figure out what you need to figure out.
In the following puzzle, start off by determining your objective and then restate the puzzle in a way that makes it easier to approach.

Three missionaries and three cannibals need to cross a river in a boat that can hold only two people. The missionaries must be careful never to allow the cannibals to outnumber them on either shore. How can everyone cross the river?

Reproduced from **Brain-Teasers for Trainers** by Graham Roberts-Phelps and Anne McDougall, Gower, Aldershot.

Precision Problem Solving

In the following puzzles each letter represents a different digit.
Can you decode the correct letter/number combinations?

```
  SEVEN          SEND          ABCDE
-  NINE        + MORE        X      4
  EIGHT         MONEY         EDCBA


   WIRE         WRONG         LETTERS
 +MORE         +WRONG       +ALPHABET
  MONEY         RIGHT         SCRABBLE
```

Reproduced from **Brain-Teasers for Trainers** by Graham Roberts-Phelps and Anne McDougall, Gower, Aldershot.

Rorschach Inkblot

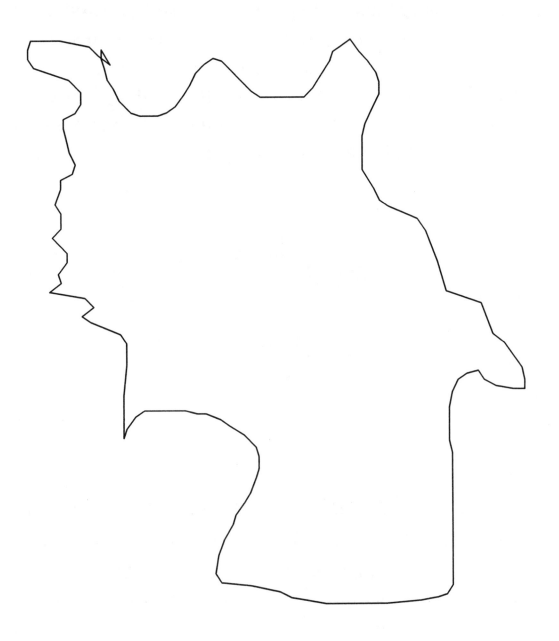

Reproduced from **Brain-Teasers for Trainers** by Graham Roberts-Phelps and Anne McDougall, Gower, Aldershot.

Life Metaphors

Visualisation and metaphors are powerful ways to gain better understanding of abstract issues.
Take a few minutes' quiet reflection to draw, represent or describe what your career or life looks like. For example, cities are often described as a 'jungle' or business life as being all 'up hill'- perhaps a race.

After 5~10 minutes, discuss your metaphors with those next to you. How does it feel if you use their metaphors instead of yours?

Training Resource ref: 76

Mental Tour ~ The Orange

Imagine that you're holding an orange.
Picture what it would feel like,
what it would look like, try to form as clear an image as
you can. Now imagine peeling off the skin,
pulling apart the segments,
and biting into a piece.

After a moment, examine a segment very closely.
Ask yourself what the orange would look like
if you could enlarge it a thousand times, or a million
times.
What might the cells look like?
What might the molecules look like?

For the next couple of minutes,
try to become aware of everything
that you know and don't know about oranges.

Think about what makes an orange an orange,
why it tastes the way it does,
how many types of oranges there may be,
how oranges may have evolved through time,
what purposes oranges may serve,
and how to make a good orange marmalade.
As you think about the orange,
pay close attention to the quality of your thoughts.

Training Resource ref: 77

Reproduced from **Brain-Teasers for Trainers** by Graham Roberts-Phelps and Anne McDougall, Gower, Aldershot.

Two~Minute Mind Tour ~ The Clock

Image that you are sitting in front of a clock or a watch that has a sweep second hand.

*Relax for a few moments,
collect your attention,
and when you're ready,
place your attention on the motion
of the second hand.*

For two minutes, focus your awareness on the movement of the second hand as if nothing else in the universe existed.

*If you lose the thread of concentration
by thinking about something else,
or just by spacing out,
stop, collect your attention,
and start again.*

*Try to keep your concentration
for two solid minutes.*

Training Resource ref: 78

Reproduced from **Brain-Teasers for Trainers** by Graham Roberts-Phelps and Anne McDougall, Gower, Aldershot.

Metattention

Look around the room and find six objects that contain circles.

Training Resource ref: 79

Visualisation/1

Almost a century ago, psychologist Francis Galton devised a
questionnaire that probed the clarity of people's imaginations.
Besides discovering that few people are true eidetic imagers,
Galton discovered that people's visualisation skills do not
improve easily. Here is a modification of his test.

Training Resource ref: 80

Reproduced from **Brain-Teasers for Trainers** by Graham Roberts-Phelps and Anne McDougall, Gower, Aldershot.

Visualisation/2

Imagine last night's dinner. Spend a minute or two picturing the scene. Visualise the people you were with, the surroundings, the table settings, the taste of the food, the sounds you heard. Before reading on, take some time to allow your image to build, piece by piece.

START NOW.

Training Resource ref: 81

Visualisation/3

✓ Is your image clear or indistinct?

✓ Is the image brighter or dimmer than the original scene?

✓ Are all parts of the scene sharply defined at the same instant, or are some parts clearer than others?

✓ Does the image appear in colour or in shades of grey?

✓ Can you form a single visual image of the entire dining room?

✓ Can you retain a steady image of your dinner plate? If so, does it grow brighter?

✓ Can you mentally see your dinner plate, your hands holding a knife and fork, a person's face sitting across from you all at the same time?

✓ Can you feel the texture of the food?

✓ Can you picture what people were wearing?

Goal Visualisation

Form a mental picture of yourself doing or having
something that you want to have or want to do.
You could picture yourself in a new suit or working at a new
job, or playing your favourite sport.
In this visualisation, three things are important:

1. Include details by engaging all of your senses.

2. Imagine yourself enjoying the scenario you wish for
   yourself.

3. Picture the scene happening on a specific date. By
   encouraging you to focus on your objectives this
   visualisation helps to stir up your motivation.

Start with a small, easy-to-reach goal and work up to larger, more encompassing goals.

Training Resource ref: 83

Reproduced from **Brain-Teasers for Trainers** by Graham Roberts-Phelps and Anne McDougall, Gower, Aldershot.

Goal Visualisation

---

1. Select your forthcoming presentation:

If you are going to give a presentation - in a sales meeting, in a speech, or in an interview - picture a range of possible scenarios. Begin with an ideal outcome.

Imagine you're performing in top shape with things happening exactly as you want them to. Then picture a mediocre outcome, with things happening close to the ideal but not quite. Then visualise the worst possible outcome with you stumbling over yourself. In the process of rehearsing these scenarios, you prepare yourself for mishaps and problems. Then once you have worked through the possibilities, focus on the ideal images. Run this movie in your mind over and over - forwards, backwards, in slow motion, as a member of the audience, through your eyes.

Be ready to contribute this image to the audience in the group discussion that follows.

Training Resource ref: 84

Reproduced from **Brain-Teasers for Trainers** by Graham Roberts-Phelps and Anne McDougall, Gower, Aldershot.

Clustering

Get a pen and a piece of paper. In the centre of the paper, write the word 'freedom'. Draw a circle around it, and jot down any thoughts, feelings and associations that you have about the idea of freedom. Record these thoughts by drawing a circle and writing one or two words inside the circle. Connect related ideas by drawing lines between them. Let your ideas branch out in every direction. Write down the ideas as quickly as you can until no more ideas come into your mind.
Allow your thoughts to go wherever they want.

START NOW

Reproduced from **Brain-Teasers for Trainers** by Graham Roberts-Phelps and Anne McDougall, Gower, Aldershot.

Caption Competition / 1

Consider the pictures below and think of witty or amusing captions or headlines.

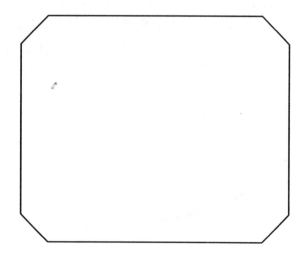

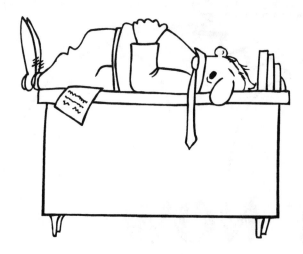

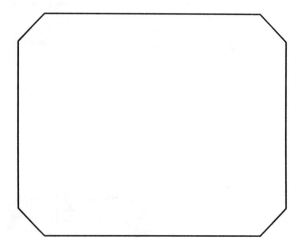

Reproduced from **Brain-Teasers for Trainers** by Graham Roberts-Phelps and Anne McDougall, Gower, Aldershot.

Caption Competition/2

Consider the picture below and think of a witty or amusing caption or headline.

Reproduced from **Brain-Teasers for Trainers** by Graham Roberts-Phelps and Anne McDougall, Gower, Aldershot.

Caption
Competition/3

Consider the pictures below and think of witty or amusing
captions or headlines.

Reproduced from **Brain-Teasers for Trainers** by Graham Roberts-Phelps and Anne McDougall, Gower, Aldershot.

Doublets Exercises

Two words are proposed of the same length, and the puzzle consists in linking these together by interposing other words, each of which shall differ from the next word in one letter only. That is to say, one letter may be changed in one of the given words, then one letter in the word so obtained, and so on, until we arrive at another given word. The letters must not be inter-changed among themselves, but each must keep its own place.

3 links

Change OAT to RYE

Close an EYE LID

4 links

Drive PIT into STY

REST on a SOFA

5 links

Go from FAST to SLOW

Take the FOOT PATH

6 links

Make WHEAT into BREAD

Show that PITY is GOOD

Reproduced from **Brain-Teasers for Trainers** by Graham Roberts-Phelps and Anne McDougall, Gower, Aldershot.

Doublets Exercises

Two words are proposed of the same length, and the puzzle consists in linking these together by interposing other words, each of which shall differ from the next word in one letter only. That is to say, one letter may be changed in one of the given words, then on letter in the word so obtained, and so on, until we arrive at another given word. The letters must not be inter-changed among themselves, but each must keep its own place.

3 links

Make HOT TEA
It's HALF TIME
Gaze at the MOON BEAM

4 links

Change a FISH into a BIRD
Fasten your LIFE BELT
Drink some PORT WINE

5 links

Take the PAWN with the KING
POOR into RICH
Make FLOUR into BREAD

6 links

Raise FOUR to FIVE
How BLACK is like WHITE

Reproduced from **Brain-Teasers for Trainers** by Graham Roberts-Phelps and Anne McDougall, Gower, Aldershot.

Anagrams/1

Reshuffle the letters of the word ASPIRANT and you can find the word PARTISAN. How long will it take you to find new words from the following list?

TREASON

WANDER

BESTIARY

MEDUSA

MASCULINE

DICTIONARY

Reproduced from **Brain-Teasers for Trainers** by Graham Roberts-Phelps and Anne McDougall, Gower, Aldershot.

Anagrams/2

Reshuffle the letters of the word ASPIRANT and you can find the word PARTISAN. How long will it take you to find new words from the following list?

DIRECTOR

CATECHISM

LEOPARD

CONSIDERATE

EXCITATION

LEGISLATOR

Reproduced from **Brain-Teasers for Trainers** by Graham Roberts-Phelps and Anne McDougall, Gower, Aldershot.

Appended Anagrams/1

Add the letter C to each of the words below, then rearrange the letters to find a new word. Add another C, resort the letters, and find yet another word. For example, add C to OIL and create COIL. Add a C to COIL and create COLIC.

SEAR   RILE   SPITE

TAPE   IRK   HEAD

ARK   NOSE   HERE

Reproduced from **Brain-Teasers for Trainers** by Graham Roberts-Phelps and Anne McDougall, Gower, Aldershot.

Appended Anagrams/2

Add the letter C to each of the words below, then rearrange the letters to find a new word. Add another C, resort the letters, and find yet another word. For example, add C to OIL and create COIL. Add a C to COIL and create COLIC.

LEAN   HAT

                        LOUT

NEAR

NEAT   HATE

Training Resource ref: 94

Alphabet Advance

If you shift each of the letters of the word COLD three positions forward, so that the letter C becomes F, O becomes R, L becomes O, and D becomes G, you arrive at a new word, FROG. In the following list of words, some must be advanced, and others reversed.

Can you figure out the other words?

TIGER   JOLLY

ADDER   FILLS

SORRY   FREUD

CHAIN   FERNS

Reproduced from **Brain-Teasers for Trainers** by Graham Roberts-Phelps and Anne McDougall, Gower, Aldershot.

Circle of Thought

Below, you are looking at an ancient stone carving of a circle of thought made by the Egyptians. How many words can you find in this circle of letters? Start at any letter and travel in a clockwise direction.

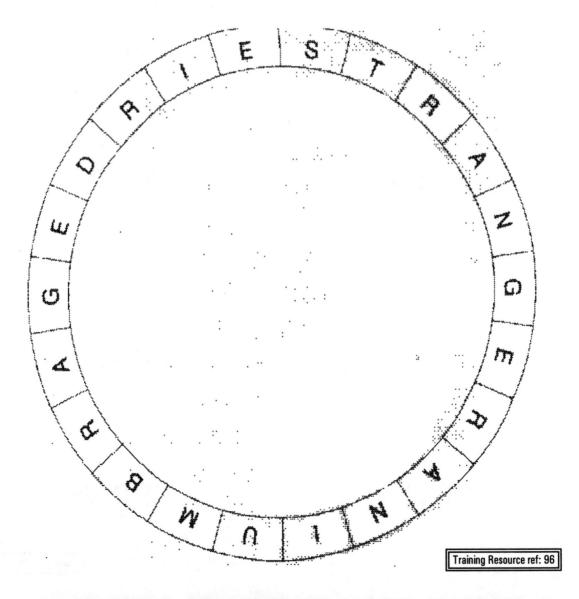

Reproduced from **Brain-Teasers for Trainers** by Graham Roberts-Phelps and Anne McDougall, Gower, Aldershot.

Spontaneous Speechmaking

As soon as you read or hear each of the following words, make four statements aloud about, around or using the word.

kettle	binderkey
program	camera
money	grid
sex	silly
sink	bats
tiger	sugar
travel	liquid
reality	ferret

Training Resource ref: 97

Reproduced from **Brain-Teasers for Trainers** by Graham Roberts-Phelps and Anne McDougall, Gower, Aldershot.

Can You Say It Another Way?/1

Human beings who have the gift of speaking have at their disposal a rich and varied vocabulary as well as the knowledge of where and when to use words. They can find the word that expresses the exact shade of meaning they wish to convey. How many words or phrases can you come up with that mean the same or almost the same as the following words? (Aim for at least ten of each.)

Foolish

Important

Sad

Friend

Fearful

Reproduced from **Brain-Teasers for Trainers** by Graham Roberts-Phelps and Anne McDougall, Gower, Aldershot.

Can you say it Another Way?/2

How many words or phrases can you come up with that mean the same or almost the same as the following words? (Aim for at least ten of each.)

Attractive

Self assured

Happy

Wonderful

Relaxed

Reproduced from **Brain-Teasers for Trainers** by Graham Roberts-Phelps and Anne McDougall, Gower, Aldershot.

Word Creation/1

Invent meanings for the following nonsense words:

Tinbucker

Presstomb

Bleesh

Emoushe

Shebarrah

Kagnst

Reproduced from **Brain-Teasers for Trainers** by Graham Roberts-Phelps and Anne McDougall, Gower, Aldershot.

Word Creation/2

Invent meanings for the following nonsense words:

Crustophenpalious

Rampithicrate

Illuspronatural

Carceptinous

Pharalpleupeian

Harmplot

Reproduced from **Brain-Teasers for Trainers** by Graham Roberts-Phelps and Anne McDougall, Gower, Aldershot.

Clear
Descriptions/1

How would you describe the following things to someone
who is entirely unfamiliar with them:

Snow

Shaking hands

How to put on a jacket

Sexual intercourse

Long multiplication

Reproduced from **Brain-Teasers for Trainers** by Graham Roberts-Phelps and Anne McDougall, Gower, Aldershot.

Clear Descriptions/2

How would you describe the following things to someone who is entirely unfamiliar with them:

The satisfaction of raking a lawn free from leaves

What your place of work looks like

Pop music

Cricket

How to do up a neck tie

Reproduced from **Brain-Teasers for Trainers** by Graham Roberts-Phelps and Anne McDougall, Gower, Aldershot.

Limerick Competition

Make up a limerick using one of the following first lines: (If you have time, produce as many as you can.)

There was once a vicar named Gus...

A travelling salesman rang twice...

A girl who weighed too much...

There was a smart lad from Madras...

There was a young man from Paris...

Reproduced from **Brain-Teasers for Trainers** by Graham Roberts-Phelps and Anne McDougall, Gower, Aldershot.

Word Power

There seems to be the right name for just about everything. Test your ability to create innovative names that grab people's attention. Make up names for the following (if time allows, create several names for each):

- ✓ a perfume
- ✓ a fashion line
- ✓ an introduction service
- ✓ a wheelbarrow
- ✓ a pop song
- ✓ a pop group
- ✓ a pet dog
- ✓ a computer company
- ✓ a new model of sports car
- ✓ a stage name for a singer

Training Resource ref: 105

Reproduced from **Brain-Teasers for Trainers** by Graham Roberts-Phelps and Anne McDougall, Gower, Aldershot.

A Funny Thing Happened...

Make up a joke or humorous story from the following subject:

- ⮑ *a funny thing happened on the way to the training course...*

- ⮑ *a traffic warden and a gorilla*

- ⮑ *an actress and a vicar*

- ⮑ *a dog walks into a pub*

- ⮑ *a salesman in heaven/hell*

- ⮑ *a political figure*

- ⮑ *a chef and a police officer*

- ⮑ *a fisherman in front of the gates of heaven.*

Training Resource ref: 106

Reproduced from **Brain-Teasers for Trainers** by Graham Roberts-Phelps and Anne McDougall, Gower, Aldershot.

Story Creation

Choose one word at random from each of the four columns, and use them as trigger concepts to construct a story. Develop the scenario on paper into a short, interesting story and be ready to present this to the group.

A	B	C	D
fizzle	ocean	travel	sandwich
wallet	watermelon	dream	motorcycle
sideline	criminal	statue	toe-nail
pavement	topcoat	veneer	charisma
army	nose	Frisbee	spiral
car	gorilla	Frenchman	table
fishing rod	banana	Yeti	goldfish
finish	button	soufflé	box
stick	steal	fruit	cowboy

Training Resource ref: 107

The Turkish Bath Mystery

Four men met every Thursday lunchtime at the Turkish baths. Joe was a musician and always brought his personal cassette player so that he could listen to music.

Jack was a banker and he always brought a thermos containing a drink.

Jim and John were both lawyers and brought paperback books to read. One day in the mist-filled room, John was found dead from a deep wound through his heart. The police were called immediately.

They questioned all three suspects, but no one said that they had seen anything happen.

A thorough search was carried out, but no murder weapon could be found. What had happened?

Training Resource ref: 108

Reproduced from **Brain-Teasers for Trainers** by Graham Roberts-Phelps and Anne McDougall, Gower, Aldershot.

Antony And Cleopatra

Antony and Cleopatra are lying dead on the floor in an Egyptian villa. Nearby is a broken bowl. There are no marks on the bodies and they were not poisoned. No person was in the villa when they died. How did they die?

Reproduced from **Brain-Teasers for Trainers** by Graham Roberts-Phelps and Anne McDougall, Gower, Aldershot.

A Remarkable Journey

In 1930, two men drove from New York to Los Angeles in a Ford motor car.

The journey of 3340 miles took 18 days to complete. This wasn't the first, fastest or slowest journey of its kind.

They drove on normal roads, the car was not remarkable and the two men were normal. But because of this journey, these two men hold a world record that endures to this day.

What is it?

Reproduced from **Brain-Teasers for Trainers** by Graham Roberts-Phelps and Anne McDougall, Gower, Aldershot.

The Abyssinian Postal Service

The Abyssinian Postal Service has a strict rule stating that items sent through the post must not be more than 1 metre long.

Longer items must be sent by private carriers, who are notorious for their expense, inefficiency, and high rate of loss of goods.

Boris was desperate to send his valuable and ancient flute safely through the post. Unfortunately, it was 1.4 metres long and could not be disassembled as it was one long, hollow piece of ebony.

Eventually he hit on a way to send it through the Abyssinian Postal Service.

What did he do?

Reproduced from **Brain-Teasers for Trainers** by Graham Roberts-Phelps and Anne McDougall, Gower, Aldershot.

The Hotel Detective

A hotel detective was walking along a corridor of a large hotel one day. Suddenly, he heard a woman's voice cry out 'For God's sake, don't shoot me John!' Then there was a shot.

He ran to the room from where the shot had come and burst in. In one corner of the room lay a woman who had been shot through the heart. In the middle of the room was a gun that had been used to shoot her.

On the other side of the room stood a postman, a lawyer and an accountant. The detective looked at them for a moment and then walked towards the postman, grabbed him, and said 'I'm arresting you for the murder of that woman.' It was, in fact, the postman who had murdered the woman, but how did the detective know?

The detective had not seen seen any of the people in the room before.

Reproduced from **Brain-Teasers for Trainers** by Graham Roberts-Phelps and Anne McDougall, Gower, Aldershot.

Concorde

A businessman had an important business meeting that led him to fly by Concorde from London to New York. When he left home in the morning, his wife drove him to the airport and accompanied him to the check-in. She then waved goodbye as he went through passport control and the departure lounge.

She did some shopping at the airport shops and returned to the car, at which time she saw the Concorde take off on time. His flight on Concorde was of course a direct flight.

When he reached New York, he went directly through immigration and customs. He had no luggage to collect as he only took a briefcase for his short trip.

He went through to the arrivals hall and there waiting for him was his wife! It was only that morning that she had seen him off.

She had not flown or taken the boat, so how could she be there to meet him?

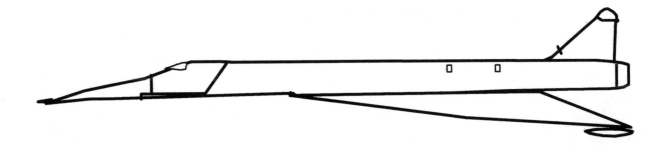

Training Resource ref: 113

World War I

A true story

At the beginning of World War I, the uniform of the British soldiers included a brown cloth cap. They were not provided with metal helmets.

As the war went on, the army authorities and the War Office became alarmed at the high proportion of men with head injuries. They therefore decided to replace all cloth headgear with metal helmets. From then on, all the soldiers wore the metal helmets.

However, the War Office was amazed to discover that the incidence of head injuries increased. It can be assumed that the intensity of fighting was the same before and after the change.

So why should the recorded number of head injuries per battalion increase when the men wore metal helmets instead of cloth caps?

Training Resource ref: 114

King George IV

A true story

King George IV was born in 1762. He was king of England from 1820 to his death in 1830.

He was not a great king, but he did start a new trend in footwear. His boots were different from everybody else's.

The innovation concerning his boots was copied and is commonplace today, but at the time was very unusual.

What was it?

Reproduced from **Brain-Teasers for Trainers** by Graham Roberts-Phelps and Anne McDougall, Gower, Aldershot.

The Dream

The boss of a storage warehouse had just arrived at work when one of his employees burst into his office.

The man explained that while asleep the previous night he had dreamed that one of the stored boxes contained a bomb that would explode at two p.m., causing a terrible fire.

The boss was sceptical but agreed to investigate. After a search, a bomb was found in the area foreseen in the man's dream. The police were called, the bomb defused, and a tragedy averted. Afterwards the boss thanked the employee sincerely, then fired him.

The sacked man had not planted the bomb, and his prophetic dream had saved the warehouse from destruction. Yet the manager was right to fire him.

How could this be so?

Training Resource ref: 116

Reproduced from **Brain-Teasers for Trainers** by Graham Roberts-Phelps and Anne McDougall, Gower, Aldershot.

The Man in the Hotel

Mr Smith and Mr Jones are two businessmen who book into the same hotel for the night.

They are given adjacent rooms on the third floor. During the night, Mr Smith sleeps soundly. However, despite being very tired, Mr Jones can't fall asleep. He eventually phones Mr Smith and falls asleep immediately after hanging up.

Why should this be so?

Training Resource ref: 117

Short Roads

There are four main towns in Squareville. We will call them A, B, C and D. They lie at the corners of a ten mile square. In order to improve communications between the towns, the Squareville Department of Transport decided to build a new road linking all four towns together. Because they had very little money, it was decided that the new road system should be as short as possible and still allow access from any one town to another. The engineers came up with three designs, shown below.

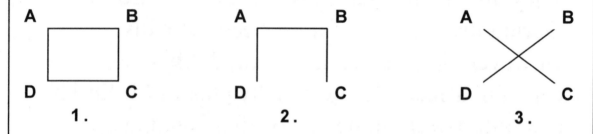

Number one uses 40 miles of road, number two uses 30 miles of road, and number three uses 28.3 miles of road. The designers naturally recommended plan three, because it employed the smallest road area, and therefore cost the least. When they showed the plans to the Minister of Finance, he accused them of extravagance and pointed out an even better design which had even less road surface.

What was it?

Training Resource ref: 118

The Plane Hijacker

A true story

A few years ago in the USA, a young man hijacked a passenger flight at gunpoint. He ordered the pilot to fly to a different airport and radioed his demands to the airport authorities.

In return for the safe release of the plane and hostages, he asked for $100,000 in a bag and two parachutes.

When the plane landed, he was given the bag and two parachutes. He then instructed the pilot to fly at a fairly low altitude towards their original destination. When they were over a deserted part of the country, he strapped on one of the parachutes and, clutching the bag of money, he leapt from the plane. The second parachute was not used. He was never found.

You have to answer one question.

Why did he ask for two parachutes if we assume that he only ever intended to use one?

Training Resource ref: 119

Games for Trainers

3 Volume Set

Andy Kirby

Most trainers use games. And trainers who use games collect new games. Andy Kirby's three-volume compendium contain 75 games in each volume. They range from icebreakers and energizers to substantial exercises in communication. Each game is presented in a standard format which includes summary, statement of objectives, list of materials required, recommended timings and step-by-step instructions for running the event. Photocopiable masters are provided for any materials needed by participants.

All the games are indexed by objectives, and Volume 1 contains an introduction analysing the different kinds of game, setting out the benefits they offer and explaining how to use games to the maximum advantage. It is a programmed text designed to help trainers to develop their own games. Volume 3 reflects current trends in training; in particular the increased attention being paid to stress management and assertiveness. Volumes 2 and 3 contain an integrated index covering all three volumes.

Gower

Outdoor Games for Trainers

Carmine Consalvo

Games are perennially popular as a training method for developing teamworking and problem-solving skills. Consalvo has collected together 63 games specifically designed for outdoor use. All of the events can be conducted easily and safely with the minimum of materials and preparation. Many of them can be run equally well indoors.

Each activity is presented in a standard format that includes a summary, a statement of objectives, a note of any materials required, approximate timings and detailed guidance on what to do, when and how, covering both content and process. The exercises vary in length from a few minutes to over an hour. Titles reflect their inventiveness, ranging from: *Space Escape* to *Shuffling the Deck*, and from *Wet Dog Wiggle* to *Ostrich Eggs*. Together they provide a rich store of adventure, energy and memorable learning.

Gower

Team Development Games for Trainers

Roderick R Stuart

If you're involved in designing interpersonal skills training you will know that there are two serious problems. The first is to find material that matches the relevant objectives. The second is to find material that will be unfamiliar to the participants.

None of the 59 games in Roderick Stuart's collection has appeared in print before. Based on the author's experience with many different types of organization and trainee, they cover the whole gamut of skills associated with team development, including assertiveness, communication, creativity, decision making, influencing, listening, planning, problem solving and time management.

Each activity is presented in a standard format, with an indication of objectives, timing and group size, and detailed step-by-step guidance for the trainer or team leader. A consolidated index makes it easy to select the most suitable items for your training need and to compile workshops or more extensive programmes. In addition the author provides a four-stage model that relates learning to the requirements of the workplace, and a set of checklists for facilitating the learning process. Altogether, a valuable resource.

Gower